The Abortionist's Vacation

Maria Andreas

www.mariaandreas.eu

Translated from the French *Les Vacances de L'Avorteur*
by Jacqueline Tobin 2025

Published by Huge Jam 2025

www.hugejam.com

First edition.

Copyright © 2025 Maria Andreas

All rights reserved.

ISBN:978-1-916604-30-8

For Mireille.
In memory of my brother
Laurent.

My gratitude to Dr. Gerard Ostermann
for his preface.

Beyond all words, to be under the gaze
of his therapy is to take one more step closer to
all kinds of remedy.

*

Thank you to Jacqueline (Huge Jam).
Once again, her talents as a translator and her
artistic sensibilities have captured in English
the depths of my heart!

"A story is not a return to the past,
It's a reconciliation with it."

Boris Cyrulnik
from *Autobiography of a Scarecrow*, Odile Jacob, 2008

Preface
Dr. Gérard Ostermann

With *The Abortionist's Vacation*, Maria Andreas offers us a work of rare intensity, where the intimate meets the universal in a tale that is at once poignant, raw, and profoundly human. Oscillating as it does between autobiography and family saga, this is much more than a simple life story: it is a dizzying plunge into the twists and turns of memory, family legacies, and the wounds that shape identity.

From the very first pages, the author captivates us with the incandescence of her writing, where caustic humor and tenderness blend with striking accuracy. The direct and powerful language leaves no respite, drawing us into a whirlwind of emotions where tragedy rubs shoulders with human comedy. Each sentence resonates with raw truth, carried by a disarming sincerity and uncompromising lucidity.

One of the great strengths of this story lies in the strength of its characters, sketched with rare psychological acuity. Suzanne, the mother with an indomitable character, pierces the reader with her fierce independence and resilience in the face of adversity. Pierre-André, the true love, embodies both passion and the pain of incomprehension. And what about Loulou, this brother with a shattered career, whose tragic destiny is recounted with moving modesty? Maria Andreas doesn't just tell the story; she brings these people back to life in all their complexity, their contradictions, and their dazzling humanity.

The story also shines with its masterful construction, alternating childhood memories, moments of tenderness, polished dialogue, and sometimes heart-breaking episodes. The author manages to capture the essence of each era she travels through, whether it's Kenya bathed in light, an Algeria vibrant with contrasts, or a Europe with its oppressive winters. The family saga is thus part of a larger story, that of exile, the search for meaning, and the silent battles fought by those often forgotten by official history.

Beyond its testimony, *The Abortionist's Vacation* is a vibrant work of life, an ode to family ties despite their cracks, a reflection on transmission and the place each person tries to find in the great mosaic of destiny. It is a text that shakes, moves, and, above all, leaves an indelible mark on the reader's heart. A book of rare power, carried by a pen that dares everything: irony, melancholy, rage, and love. Essential.

Dr. Gérard Ostermann

*Professor of Therapeutic
Internal Medicine – Psychotherapist (ARS)
EMDR Practitioner Europe*
https://www.gerardostermann.fr

A few years before his death, I was having lunch in a Parisian restaurant with my old friend, Monsignor Germain, whose humour and instinct for banter had remained intact despite his age. I wanted, before one of us entered fools' paradise, to remind him of my affection, despite our paths no longer crossing. I said to him:

"You know, there are idiots everywhere!"

With his Anglo-Saxon phlegm, he replied:

"Yes ... and that includes us!"

1
She Was 15

"I'll finish washing her, Madam, just give me a few more minutes!"

A young care assistant in a hurry to finish his shift. As I close the door, I see what comes next, her night shirt raised to the navel, thighs wobbling slightly. He stands there with a glove and a small basin.

He judges it an indecent thing that I should assist in the sloppy protocol of the slit's ablutions. That dry sex that I was conceived in about sixty years ago. I wonder how I managed to get out ...

He doesn't speak. I hear him rinsing his basin:

"Do you want to clean your teeth?"

"No, it's okay, not tonight!" She doesn't want clean teeth, she wants to chat. Because, despite the effects of a stroke that was never treated, she has held onto a dazzling repertoire of anecdotes, hilarious to those bawdy enough to take them. Not to mention the spiritual lessons a life of quests has armed her with. She is rather malicious in homing in on her interlocutor, who keeps looking at his phone:

"Tonight after work, will you be getting a blow job?"

"But that's none of your business, Mrs Favre-Bulle!"

"In any case, my husband was one hell of a shooter!"

"But that's none of my business, Mrs Favre-Bulle!"

"I'm telling you anyway! Often three times a night!"

I didn't think my male progenitor capable of such prowess! I am split between laughter and embarrassment as I find her in her bed with Moutzi, the teddy bear that her granddaughter Mireille had given her. Her Moutzi, her emotional refuge since Dad's death the year before. He reminds her of her first love, the Mani figure of her Dickensian childhood. He was in tatters when we had to throw him out, as – being so in need of cuddles – she had kept him crushed against her chest like a child ...

I contemplate her. She is beautiful.

Angelic...

Hungry for my complicity, she changes her register and draws from her religious repertoire. Hers:

"My darling, you know why we call the Virgin *Queen of the skies?*"

"No Mummy, tell me."

"Because she's always dribbling..."

I take her hand, I smile at her. Her unorthodox response, reflecting her almost inborn defiance, moves me. I like the authenticity of her heartfelt sharing. As Mireille keeps saying:

"Grandma couldn't care less about being loved or rejected. She says what she thinks. Period."

Toughness that didn't make her life easy. But she was able to shoulder it thanks to the unconditional support of my father, and the steadfast foil of his much more open outlook.

An episode in Costa Blanca, while the aforementioned stroke was being diagnosed in a

Spanish clinic, reveals the depth of their consuming love. A brain scan had been prescribed. Paperwork detailing the dangers of the substances to be injected was handed to them in the waiting room, explaining that an allergy could be triggered in the worst, fatal scenarios. My father relayed their conversation to me:

"We should read it ..."

"Shall I sign it, Pierre?"

"My love, you're alive, and that's the only thing that matters! Come on, let's get out of here!"

And they went out to drink a good milky coffee on an Alicante terrace.

It was then that the sharpshooter, with a self-sacrifice that kicked back against the tiniest of setbacks, made another one of his life choices. To cherish her for more than another ten years, until his own life force was exhausted.

Yes, they gazed at each other ...

They always gazed at each other. Until the last gaze, 73 years after that first lightning bolt.

He was 16, she was 15.

A teenager forced to grow up early:

"With an unhinged mother, I had to get my ass

in gear real fast!"

She wasn't rude but she'd use rude words without any qualms. Ones that released enough energy to allow her to get her feelings out. Rather than suffocate...

As a little girl, she'd spent her weekends at the cemetery. My grandmother's fiancé had been killed in a skiing accident three weeks before their wedding, and the deranged girl could never bring herself to move away from that grotesquely named final resting place. That grave where her James was encrusted, as my mother had called it, repulsed by voracious maggots on dead bodies.

However, one day Bluette met a cop – such a fittingly professional term for my grandfather – who came across as so self-assured. Bluette quickly became attached to him; a widower with a three-year-old child. Impressed by his future in-laws' impeccable housekeeping, the cop proposed in record time. But, not only had the in-laws, whose home was indeed polished to the nines, not considered it useful to teach their daughter a trade, they had never required her to do any household chores. At the beginning of the 20th century, the fate of a vestal virgin – who, they fantasised, was beautiful enough to have been of noble birth – had embraced little progress. So her education was focused on reading, decorative crafts, and learning to play the piano. Resulting in her having ambitious exhibitions in that working-class town in French-speaking Switzerland, while her three brothers worked in the small family workshop.

It seems that the honeymoon was a disaster. A disaster at the origin of my own life, as the two protagonists decided to have a baby whose mission was all about bringing them closer together.

My mother's birth, four years before the Crash of 1929, turned out to be one of her rare mission failures. Six months later, the self-assured cop abandoned the messy home and the Crazy Woman and scrawny baby whose first betrayal was that of being a female. Into his suitcase went his framed lucky mascot. An icon of the adored first wife. An Adored One who was all the more sublime for being dead, after giving birth to equally dead twins…

With this panoply of deaths, my mother had no choice but to escort this German – who, as a bonus, had the nerve to be called Adolphe – to Rose's tomb. Rose the Perfect. Rose the Irreplaceable, encrusted with her two miscarried cop larvae for company.

Shaken by the curse of divorce, a word as filthy as a dirty word, the Crazy Woman, crazier by the minute, retreated into the parental home with its polished nooks and crannies. And Suzanne became the only kid in her circle to have a name different from her mother's. An anomaly that her first teacher, with her embittered virginity, analysed regularly in front of the whole class.

Suzanne…

The German had wanted to call her Rose, which might have aroused a little paternal affection. But he hadn't counted on the obsessive desire of the Adored One's legitimate child to obliterate her half-sister, by any means possible, from the family records. The intolerable heartbreak of losing a mother had not engendered a desire to share anything with a younger sister. As for the cop, finding himself caught between the Crazy Woman's daughter and the Irreplaceable One's daughter, his choice was as instantaneous as it was definitive.

However, the eight years that followed were the most bearable for Suzanne. Thanks to the love of her grandmother, who juggled between wearing her bookkeeping hat at the small workshop, her polishing hat at home and her teaching hat with her granddaughter. Bluette, adrift in depression, even gave up her piano. And little by little sank into a pathological bulimia. In this sleepy working-class town where psychotherapy rhymed with lunatic asylum, this odd behaviour was described, more out of ignorance than malice, as gluttony. Crazy and gluttonous, the stifled vestal virgin had no choice but to choke on anything that seemed edible to her. To the point of keeping watch on the pavement for when her little girl brought back the sweet bricelets her father made so she could snatch a cone and devour it before going back in. Or even devouring six meringues in the stairwell. This pathology worsened when it was associated with chronic insomnia. The crazy glutton would get up at night to lay waste to the food cupboards. I have just gone through an episode that forced me to glimpse my grandmother's hell. Insomnia for five nights in a row, following an infection that was treated with cortisone injections among other things. In the middle of the fifth night, I made myself some porridge to soothe my gastritis. I remembered then that it was one of the dishes, if not the only dish, cooked by the crazy gluttonous insomniac. Exhausted and beside myself, I lay back down and brushed against that fatal blade above me, below me, beyond me and within me. The tipping point…

Bluette, the madwoman, the glutton, the insomniac, was simply ill. I had known it but I had just verified it through my own tortured flesh, that was in turn torturing the soul as if to relieve itself. A posthumous communion adding meaning to my own self-neglect and to the week-long, hellish virus.

As for the real ordeal, it started its attack on the polished hearth when my great-grandmother Bertha's health showed the first signs of exhaustion. However, that year, she spared none of her energy in giving little Suzanne one last magical Christmas. All her life, Mother would talk about the smells, the decorations, but especially the lights. On the tree, the lights. Those lights that transported her child's gaze to a paradise without a lunatic, without an inconsolable Adolphe, without an inquisitive virgin, without a plotting sister and without maggots!

Despite the multiple laying on of hands by a charismatic street sweeper who, in this period of global disarray, had just founded the equally charismatic sect of the New Apostles, Bertha's condition worsened. In March, when the snow melted, the light from the polished hearth escaped into every nook and cranny forever. Collapse was general, even the cat began to whine incessantly. For Suzanne, the Apocalypse prophesied by the charismatic street sweeper had just crushed the only safe space in her fragmented heart. She recalled only one memory:

"I went out into the garden, picked a bunch of snowdrops and placed them on the coffin."

She was eight years old...

As a bad event often needs its own playmates, the family business did not survive the crisis of the Thirties. The brothers, Bluette, and their father

Émile and the cat, had to leave the home that had once been polished to the nines. The tribe was dispersed. Two of the boys to Geneva, Bluette and her daughter to a freezing basement, Émile to another of those ratholes, with toilets at the bottom of the garden. Only the cat found happiness there. Rats to chase away, a half-open skylight for his amorous escapades, all the while bringing comfort with his energetic purrs, the ultimate refuge of all tenderness. Boudi, the only one resisting that tsunami of desolation, became a hero. Until the end, Boudi's repertoire of antics brightened Suzanne's stories.

She did, however, experience a few rays of consolation in Geneva, during her only vacation with her Uncle Marcel, Bluette's younger brother. Along with his delightful wife, Joséphine. Marcel had met Joséphine, a few years older than him, just after the Second World War. They "went steady" as they said at the time, but Joséphine had been keeping all her Sundays secretly booked out. One day, she confided in him the reason for her absences. She was an abandoned single mother and had been forced to place her daughter in an orphanage.

"What? You have a child and you're only telling me now? We'll go get him right away!"

This is how little Valentine grew up with an adoptive father, and how Joséphine, eternally grateful, married this big kid for the worst. This clown, as caring as he was alcoholic, incapable of taking responsibility for himself. She worked in a factory, while Marcel took care of the child, the housework, the garden and the unfulfilled fantasies of the woman next door. All the while showering the two neglected girls with his paternal affection. As well as his niece Suzanne whom he rather dangerously taught to swim in the Rhône. He also passed on to her laughter. That antidote to adversity that Mum would cultivate all her life. Thank you, Marcel! And thank you to you too, Joséphine. Mum expressed her gratitude to you with her many visits. So it is that I see you both again. You, a handsome, defeated old man with a scarlet face, cigarette in your mouth. Tirelessly clownish and generous. You, a dignified old lady with a serene face. Serenity having taken on a *destiny* that could only seem like a privilege to you.

And so it was, because you had chosen to live it with that love radiating to the end.

Misery did not spare the Swiss beggars during those jobless years. They washed with cold water, they cut up sheets of newspaper for toilet paper, they took wood from the forest to warm themselves and they washed everything that needed washing in the kitchen sink.

Mum, though never hungry, was only to wear her first new clothes with her first salary. Before that, because the older one preferred to throw her clothes away rather than see them on her younger daughter who'd had the cheek to be pretty, they got them from a council clothes bank. A scene took place there that revealed Bluette's big mouth, the only defence she could ever call upon. Suzanne had just been given her share of second-hand clothes. Before leaving, Bluette spotted a navy-blue coat, roomy enough to encompass her plumpness:

"This coat looks great on me, I'll take it!"

"Mrs. Delapraz, you got what you agreed on. I'm sorry, you must put this coat back in its place!"

"Okay, so listen to me carefully, I'm working

my ass off raising my kid all by myself, and if I'm not even allowed to clothe myself, I'll leave her with you, you can sort it out!"

And she left with the coat ... equivalent to Suzanne in value!

Reinvigorated once out on the pavement, she didn't disappoint in drawing from her catalogue of funny faces to imitate the astonished employee. That's when they came across the charismatic street sweeper.

No doubt dazzled by the beautiful coat, he insisted that Bluette come and listen to him preach. The following Sunday, mother and daughter found themselves on the benches of the New Apostles. Hoping to escape all kinds of despair, in a world that was filled with all types of outcasts. The long-sought-after space from which to shout out loud – always the same shout – that the only person responsible went by the name of Satan. But that now, there was a way out: to take refuge body and riches, especially the riches, under the wings of God's fire being transmitted to the New Apostles:

"Lord, what my heart desires is your fire, it's

your fire, it's your fire!

"*Make us new apostles, by your fire, by your fire, by your fire...*"

Decades later, with her life-saving humour, Mum was still singing us the choruses by heart. Though it had been one of the most sordid of periods and had almost cost her her life. Bluette had let herself be transported, supported, drawn in. As is often the case in these episodes, more out of dismay than conviction. She had found someone with a bigger mouth than herself, a fiery community and above all she could finally put a name to her insomnia, her depressions, and what would become her hallucinations. For the Prince of Darkness, enraged by the zeal of this new apostle, began to torment her nights. Restless, she moaned in her bed, and when her little girl asked her what was happening, she answered: "The devil keeps pulling on my duvet!"

Neither Boudi nor Émile the Cartesian, a long-time member of the Union Circle, could stop the ship from going down. Suzanne no longer slept, Bluette soliloquised night and day, and the Charismatic One yelled even louder. One Sunday, he even attacked the pre-teenager who had dared to blaspheme by wearing a little lipstick: "This creature, my dear brothers and sisters, is possessed by Satan!" The classic refrain that would never stop Suzanne from wearing even more lipstick. All her life, even on the beach, even in the sea, a perpetual emblem of her rebellion. It was then that Émile imposed himself on what remained of his vestal virgin. She had to work, no matter what the Charismatic One or the Prince of Darkness thought. So she would do a technical apprenticeship, while he would take care of his granddaughter. And my grandmother, once she was active again, became a renowned technician.

But that time had not yet come, because of an endless succession of hallucinatory episodes. At the same time, Mum began to suffer from frequent abdominal pain. So much so that the Charismatic One discerned, in her suffering, the right moment for the laying on of hands of all the holy new apostles. Gathered to exorcise the demon from her flesh. A trauma that almost cost her her life, when a few years later, in the middle of Kenya, acute peritonitis broke out. But above all, it sealed in her soul an incurable hatred of even the most minute obscurantism...

To crown her apostolate, Bluette began to entertain suicidal thoughts that would never again leave her. One day, after dragging her chair in front of the oven with its door wide open, she turned on the gas tap, before going to inform the neighbour of her plan. This is how Bluette got transported to the insane asylum that, when mentioned in relation to the wife of an important industrialist, was called a rest home. And the state declared Suzanne fit for the orphanage. It was only in the last months of her life that I learned of this episode, Mum miming it from her council flat armchair:

"My grandfather, the clever old fox, dry as a nail took me by the hand. We went to the council, and he banged his fist on the desk:

"Her orphanage is at home with me!"

Case closed. Suzanne found some respite with Boudi and Bertha's kind husband. She paid tribute to him all her life. He died in her arms, his prostate so big that he screamed when he urinated. Surgery didn't yet provide relief like it does today! We often forget this when we only focus on the negative aspects of our time. With this "clever old fox", Suzanne was introduced to the great philosophers including her favourite, Voltaire, the herald against all forms of intolerance. And to La Fontaine's fables too, reciting them to us throughout our childhood. To literature, to painting, and especially to music. My great-grandfather's repertoire intoxicated her. His humour too, his liveliness, his courage. She loved school and she was brilliant. Except in writing and organisation, which placed her with the dunces at the back of the class. Regardless of that, she was accepted unconditionally into the secondary school, called at that time a *pro gymnase*.

Alas, Bluette, sufficiently rested from her stay in the funny farm, was full of the energy needed to oppose that intellectual destiny. To the point of sending the *gymnase* headteacher packing, when he came to find her in her hovel to convince her that school would help her daughter to go up in the world. This frustration would eat away at Mum all her life, despite a self-taught rage that would lead her to finish her career as a bilingual

PA. Bravo my darling mum, bravo! As for Adolphe, he refused to oppose the will of the Crazy One, judging it enough that the Still Adored One's daughter was undertaking studies. I'm sure it's never too late to vomit up these knots that continue to choke us regardless of the time passed.

One Sunday, arriving at the rest home early, a very committed nursing assistant was doing a sort of group therapy and Mum surprised the whole gathered community. Each of the speakers mentioned their parents. I waited in the shadows, seeing Mum slumped in her wheelchair. She seemed to be dozing, indifferent to the stories of her roommates. And then suddenly, she straightened up and shouted with as much calm as clarity:

"My parents were idiots! Both of them!"

It was early on that her child's body transformed into that of a young woman. A very beautiful young woman. Long ashen curls, the German's blue eyes, a model's waist supported by endless legs. Bluette did not only feel pride, but she also deciphered in this grace the opportunity to escape their rathole for good. Her plan could be summed up in four words:

"Make old men squirt!"

At that time, as in all times, there was no shortage of old men willing to shoot their load in front of youth and beauty. It was then that the conflict between mother and daughter crystallised into something more violent. Determined that no one should be coughing up for her precious flower, Mum would say to herself with each ominous approach:

"You won't get me, you bunch of pigs!"

Despite her contempt for the opposite sex, Bluette granted a little pleasure to her own bulimic flesh by taking a lover. A married boor who liked to growl at Suzanne:

"When are we getting rid of your slutty kid?"

Fortunately, she could count on the support of Émile, who not only introduced her to the piano but offered to accompany her one evening to a concert by a famous pianist. Seventh heaven for someone who had become a classical music enthusiast. That evening, however, she was to have a date with another passion. Her life's passion...

During the interval, she saw a young man as

dark as she was blonde, with a pale complexion and a shy smile, walk towards the empty piano. Without anyone making a request, he began to play a piece by Chopin. So it was Chopin who invited the beautiful flower, that no pig would ever possess, to rush forward and congratulate that young talent. Both as clumsy as each other, the two kids knew instantly that:

It was what it was…

It was going to turn everything upside down, transfigure everything forever! A few days later, they crossed paths on the only avenue in that still sleepy working-class town. It was he who approached her:

"Together, we are going to accomplish great things!"

She would never forget that first declaration.

She was 15 years old…

2

He Was 16

If Suzanne's parents had behaved like "idiots", Pierre-André's had bled themselves dry so that their only son could get through those years of crisis all but unscathed. Even if there was very little to bleed. In his own words:

"There was never hunger, there was never cold, but there was never surplus either!"

My grandparents were the king and queen of parsimony. A value that would accompany Dad all his life. Finishing the jar of jam even if mouldy or eating yogurts after their best before date, that "scam invented by supermarkets"! There was absolutely no doubt in his mind, and this was the source of a stifled rebellion, that a proper existence would have been a life outside of the sectarian shackles their extremely strict religious community imposed on him. With its non-negotiable respecting of the Sabbath from sunset on Friday evening.

Despising it would be akin to being friends with the devil for eternal damnation. But, in those days, other people were working Saturdays and going to classes on Saturdays. So, the rare jobs that my grandfather André could have got were given to those who did not request such flexibility. Above all, and until his last days this was a weeping sore for Pierre-André who had wanted to become a surgeon, he couldn't go to university. Luckily, the director of the watchmaking college agreed that he need not take Saturday lessons. Despite his absences, he graduated cum laude and finished his career as a technical director. A fierce worker, he took on continuous training all his life. Bravo to you too Dad! But before the successes, the boy had to watch his unemployed father crying at the table every day, and his friends graduating from top universities...

The unknotting doesn't stop there. In fact, it began long before that. Aline, his mother, the eldest of 13 children, had also had to give up her dream of becoming a teacher so as to raise her brothers and sisters. She slept in an attic that had a large waterfall in the middle of it from the water that ran off the roof on rainy days. She was expected to help on the farm and later ran the family workshop brilliantly. By the time the business had made her a well-to-do woman, it was passed on to her younger brother, deemed the only worthy successor. All the more worthy because he preached in church. It would seem he preached better than he shared. Not only did Aline not receive a penny, but years later, as she was lugging her shopping bags home, he drove right past her in his Alfa Romeo, no invitation to relieve the two arms that had swaddled him.

As far back as I can remember, I've never encountered such a gloomy being. As if he embodied all the sin in the world, from which he had to free himself through Sabbaths and deprivation, without neglecting the salutary duty of tithing. Also, as far back as I can remember, never once have I heard my grandmother complain about, much less utter the slightest criticism of, anyone. However, I must have been nine years old the day someone came to tell her of her younger brother's death:

"Aren't you sad, Grandma? Aren't you crying?"

"No, I'm not crying."

Not another syllable...

As for my grandfather André, the abundance of his childhood was also sacrificed on the altar of fanaticism. His father Léon had a small clock factory that worked well enough for his only son, very gifted at drawing, to design the models the company produced. The home was run by maids directed by Martha, my great-grandmother, from the deep confines of her wheelchair. Not quite paralysed enough to escape permanent spinal torture. During the Great Depression, again, prophet-mongers multiplied. The main prophecy being that this chaos preceded the end of the world. In a word, the victory of the rewarded chosen! While young André wanted to go to Paris to the Beaux-Arts, he was told that one did not exile oneself to the capital of perdition the day before the coronation of the righteous.

An even more significant dialogue was related to me by an old aunt. André fancied a language study trip to England: "But André, what good will it do you to learn English given that Christ is about to return?" Thus, young André learned nothing at all, for in the kingdom, it would all have proved useless.

When unemployment forced most factories to close, convinced that the end was imminent, Léon refused to pay the dues that would allow him to remain the boss of his company, dispossessing himself of what he had spent his life building. This self-denial reached its peak when a particularly zealous preacher recommended that his flock part with all jewellery or other adornments. Those too common signs of a pride that would offend the One about to descend in glory. One brooch, the only one of Martha's brooches, was saved. I still have it. As for the Apocalypse, it slipped further and further into the background. Poverty, on the other hand, without reneging on any tithe payments, came to the fore…

Nevertheless, my father adored his paternal grandparents. Affectionate, even cheerful despite the portents. But he was terrified of his maternal grandfather, a nagging and uncompromising pastor who, between sermons, found time to climb on top of his little wife and get her pregnant 13 times.

Thanks to his second cousins, Henri and Roland, Pierre-André managed to have a decent childhood. Their two mothers were sisters, while their fathers were first cousins. The more or less explicit rule was to marry within the chosen clan. Dad adored his mother, who reciprocated, and gave him enough freedom to cycle around Switzerland or learn to swim in the Doubs. Alas, despite the postponement of the Apocalypse, straying from the environs of the parish was unthinkable, something he felt an aversion bordering on violence to. Too shackled by it to realise that it had bequeathed him an exemplary sense of honesty. He ranted at the catechism. He ranted at the parish primary school. And he suffered hell at the community dentist, who proceeded to knock out his already wobbly teeth. The days, nights, weeks, months, and years passed to the rhythm of sermons and prohibitions. The slightest pleasure was suspected of sabotaging his chances of salvation. As for his marital future, it was tacitly mapped out. His second cousin proved sufficiently fervent as to do the trick. Without suspecting that this would lead her nephew into extra-parochial love affairs, his aunt, the youngest of the 13, expressed her gratitude to Aline by giving her the family piano and paying for regular lessons for Pierre-André.

His first fan was also his first and last love...

At 15, it was time for Suzanne to begin a sales apprenticeship, having failed at helping old men squirt. At 16, Pierre-André had time to perpetuate the ancestral tradition by becoming a watchmaker. Before achieving those great things, dates between them were sporadic. Then one day, she had to explain to Bluette that she was in love, irrevocably resolved to live with her love until death do them part. But this son of a penniless unemployed man didn't meet the criteria. While Bluette was forced to tolerate him, she never loved him. The complete opposite of Émile, whose verdict was summed up in a single sentence: "He's a great guy, he'll make you happy!"

Even Adolphe, despite his elder daughter having decreed that no man would ever deserve her greatness, was delighted with this choice from the very first meeting. André and Aline, for their part, opened their arms to this Giotto Madonna, convinced that they would soon lead her to the steps of the baptismal pool...

3
The Wedding Photo

Or was it of a funeral?

Aline, André, a handful of guests, Adolphe, a hard-hearted cop by definition, looked ready to follow the hearse. Bride and groom each as pale as the other. Moving with a fragility, he entirely in black, she in multitudinous veils that she had embroidered by hand. Yet the two "lost arch-virgins" as Mum loved to describe them, cared not one jot about their salvation. No baptismal pool for the Madonna, who warned everyone before the wedding that never again would she cross the foyer of a chapel. As for her beloved, he took the opportunity to leave that antechamber of paradise now that he had hit the age of consent. Aline was balanced enough in her faith to allow her motherly love to subsume her disillusionment, but André never recovered. He became engulfed in a stubborn anxiety that absolutely destroyed all dialogue with his son. To darken further the funeral-marriage conceit, the two "lost arch-virgins" had just concluded a contract with a shady businessman who was looking for a clock repairer in Kenya. In short, instead of winning a daughter and faithful convert, André and Aline lost their only son! The flight would take off 15 days after the wedding. As for Bluette, who wasn't invited to the wedding for fear of scandal, she would have to make do without this offspring who ultimately had brought her only disappointments. Adolphe took the opportunity to fall seriously ill. As a bedridden father was no longer of any interest to the Abundantly Pampered One, Suzanne spent the two weeks before her departure at his bedside. She says she found him again or, rather, found him at the moment that she left him. They would never see each other again …

March 1947, when the world was still simmering with atrocities, a deafening old bomber crossed the Alps between two air pockets. On board, a couple no longer "virgin" but still "arch-lost", infatuated with each other and with freedom.

An argument with the Kenyan businessman held them back in Cairo for a few weeks. While the Shady One settled the bill, the two newlyweds took the opportunity to satiate themselves with everything. Not least with the multiple loads shot during tempestuous nights in the country's capital city, which they had the enchantment of discovering on the backs of camels. The photos from this first stage reveal faces that are radiant and already less lost...

4
Kenya

The completion of their deflowering was set in motion from the very moment they set foot on that ochre-red earth with its fiery perfumes. The moral constraints, prohibitions, funereal expressions were destroyed, sometimes without even their knowledge. Without having endured the Apocalypse, the two lovers were propelled to Paradise. This is the term they both used to describe their lives in Nairobi. Ratholes gave way to a villa with a large garden in which they could eat all year round, with four boys to serve them. One took care of the cleaning, the other of the kitchen, the third worked in the garden. The fourth, trained by Dad, assisted him in the watchmaking workshop, while Mum took care of the shop they had opened after losing money to the Shady One. Very quickly one of the boys, the cook, stood out thanks to his qualities and his loyalty. So Mum offered to combine meals, cleaning and gardening into one role. So he could get three wages. He laughed and declined the offer, preferring to spend his own time parading freely in his long robes. With their boys, Pierre-André and Suzanne discovered the natural life that had so delighted Rousseau. But above all, no offence to the distant colonisers, they learned to laugh with their staff. Quickly initiated into Swahili, they became familiar with the universe of Kenyans whose families and women lived as naked as before the Fall. Mum told me about this exchange she'd had with her boy who, after a year of absence from his family, had gone back to spend his vacation in his home village:

"I have a new child, it's a girl, I'm happy!"

"But... you haven't been home for a year, how can you have a child?"

"It's my wife's child, so it's mine!"

Regarding this strong, tough guy, one day he provoked mad laughter among the tea guests. He'd done the laundry and then, with his accomplices, in the garden he'd hung out the condoms that dad had collected together, so that they didn't return from their nightly excursions with syphilis.

It has to be added that the daily tea guests were not choirboys. Four or five backpackers of every or no nationality landed in Shangri-La, was how my father described them. Among them, a cleptomaniac Swiss who had mastered no fewer than seven languages. He couldn't help but nick the ashtray from the dining room, the teaspoon from the tearoom, unnecessary objects that, laughing, he stuffed into his pockets. Winzler! His name resonates in my memory since the cleptomanic adventurer saved Suzanne's life. Basically one evening, after the regulars had taken leave, she felt tired and decided to leave the swimming pool. Then she collapsed through throwing up. A violent pain burning her stomach. No car, no phone and the hospital too far away to make it there. It was then, the only time that he had ever sensed such a thing, that our cleptomaniac with seven languages confided in his friends:

"...an intuition that something was wrong!"

He immediately drove Mum, writhing with

pain, and Dad writhing with dread, to the British clinic, where the distraught surgeon had to cut open, from top to bottom, the belly that had carried me. Peritonitis from a ruptured ulcer, despite the Charismatic One's exorcisms! Mum was spared, Winzler was adulated, and Dad was the most brilliant of nurses. Because years later with the help of his watchmaker's tweezers and magnifying glass, he was still removing stitches from the large scar on his beloved's belly.

Of course, life was more perilous than it would have been in their native city of watchmakers. Dad slept with a revolver under his pillow, and Mum never ventured out alone without a weapon. However, these were only used for shooting the snakes in the garden that would surround the screaming cat and dog.

My mother, confirmed autodidact, made her own dresses, the boys' robes and was soon making clothes for their new friends' daughter. A family of wealthy Hindus who headed a cereal bar business. With them and their little princess, they not only discovered Kenya by car, but also Hindu culture and cuisine. One day, the businessman proposed introducing my father to the circle of the Faithful of Aga Khan, thanks to which their watchmaking store would be sure to grow tenfold. Fearing that they might be launching themselves into a new sect, my parents declined this opportunity. Just as Dad had refused British citizenship, a prior condition for becoming the clock repairer for the entire Royal Navy. Wanting nothing that hampered their independence.

And in any case, life was so delicious! Six hours at the store before the swimming pool, tea served by boys, getaways, thrilling meetings, landscapes beyond all splendour. The best of all being devoted to carnal frenzies during those tropical nights. The incomplete contraception of that time, combined with the virtuosity of the sharpshooter, resulted in Mum having to come under the care of the British abortionist several times. It wasn't yet the time to start a family. Especially since Mum was taking secretarial and English lessons. Even if the situation was starting to get tense, as in all the colonies, they were resolved to hold onto their Shangri La for life.

A new load was shot a little too ardently,

renewing Mum's need for the famous abortionist. I will never forget this particular evening from my childhood. The moon was full. We could see it through the frosty windows of this less sleepy working-class city. Mum was tucking us in for the night as usual:

"There was a full moon the night that Dad and I decided to make Loulou!"

"Loulou" being the nickname she gave my younger brother Laurent.

"And me, when did you decide to have me?"

She hesitated, but true to form, didn't lie:

"We didn't want a child right then... but... the abortionist was on vacation."

The pregnant moon didn't flinch. She herself had no idea exactly when the sharpshooter's fastest sperm had by chance attached itself to that blissful egg that was just waiting for it...

As if to legitimise her sudden revelation, Mum continued:

"We had a magical vacation. By the sea, in Mombasa. Our first vacation. We actually spent all our savings on it. Mombasa, what a wonder! We had never seen so many lights. And the nights on the beach, with the stars reflected in the waves. Besides... the abortionist was taking his vacation in Mombasa too. So we decided to open our arms to a family. We even found you a brilliant Kenyan nanny."

Instead of the nanny arriving, troubles broke out. Despite the growing political and social turmoil around them, Mum and Dad would have dug in their heels and stayed there without hesitation, but after their neighbour's murder, they didn't want to expose their unborn baby to danger. Moreover, they had been burgled three times, left unable to return the watches that had been in for repair. So they decided to leave their paradise and try their luck in Algeria. When the plane took off, carrying their sobs far from that paradise that would always be, until their last breaths, the icon of their best years, they were no longer completely lost, much less virgins, and soon to be parents...

5
Algeria

La blanche.

Algeria the white, the whitened, the illuminated-by-the-Mediterranean-sun.

New scents, new dwellings, new echoes but also a new culture. No more pre-Lapsarian nudity! We could barely distinguish the women's kohled eyes from under their veils. Graceful or distorted silhouettes faded, hooded in the jilabas.

Suzanne, a feminist before her time, understood that here, a child conceived from sperm that hadn't come from the master of the enslaved females, would jeopardise its mother's life. The rules had changed. Natural life systematically dulled. She immediately felt hemmed in by the shimmering country with its triggering minarets. Like the apostles of a culture she'd rejected, just as she'd rejected what had haunted her childhood nights. Especially since, from the age of 25, the rebel had not been tightening her light flowing dresses, made in Paradise. As a result her two pretty buttocks and her two pretty breasts were covered with blue, from being pinched while taking buses in that lackadaisical *blanche*.

Dad for his part was animated by much less carnate concerns. To hunt down one of the country's rare rental apartments, as well as watches that had thoughtfully chosen to go on strike. For the first few months, they rented a room from a French landlady. Dad repaired watches in their room. Mum resumed her secretarial lessons, while I became familiar with it all in utero. Years later, when I placed my *pied-noir* foot back in North Africa, I instantly felt an unexpected complicity with the chant of the minarets. I could tell that I had already heard it, from the bottom of my placenta.

As soon as the temperature allowed, they spent their free time at the beach. I always thought that one of the reasons why I only feel good in the sea. Because they were the only times when Mum was breathing freely. She was still swimming in the waves the day before my birth. That day, as sparkling as the others, her waters broke at dawn. But she made it on foot to the clinic at Oranger, supported by her beloved. The doctor diagnosed that it would be a complicated birth. Towards the evening, he warned my father that a c-section would be best. Isolated and tormented, Dad was left to weigh the most cruel scenarios up against each other. Beginning with working out how they would pay for the surgery. Finally, the birth attendant decided that he would proceed with an epidural, and that he would try to extract the baby with forceps. Wager successful, I got out with two scratches to my lips. A golden evening in May, with the minaret calling for prayer. As for the worst scenario, he had to wait until Mum woke up for that one:

"My darling, we have a daughter, our little Mireille!"

"Thank you, sir. You must tell my father; he'll be pleased!"

A shock to the system! Not only had the German died several years earlier, but Dad wasn't a "sir", he was the father and the adored husband!

This amnesia lasted long enough for the sharpshooter to experience the first days of my birth as hell. However, their love, more resilient than the shock, helped Suzanne regain her senses, and the trio returned to the landlady's house. Since I was born jaundiced, she doused me with spoonfuls of *Vichy Célestin* water, which has remained one of my favourite drinks. By chance, my parents found a two-room ground floor apartment with a small garden. This corner of land – my land, because I had just received French nationality – housed me during those Algerian spring days.

Life was as organised as it could be. Mum attended classes during the day and took care of me at night, but didn't breastfeed me. She felt this method was archaic. Disgusted by the memory of scratched and mangled African breasts. Dad worked in his workshop at night. He prepared my bottles and changed my nappies during the day, before taking me for a walk in the Jardin d'Essai. Under the tender gaze of the jilabas who imagined that only a widower could take such care of his orphan. Whenever my crying exhausted them, my Moses basket would end up at the bottom of the small garden. It was there that one evening, the two young parents, back from town, discovered a large paving stone had landed next to it, luckily to the side of my tiny head. Immediate move, regardless of the cost, to the sixth floor with a large balcony where no paving stone would bury my whining. It was my turn to be as naked as before the Fall, savouring my first months in the great outdoors. Night and day. With my only companions the smells and sounds that I soak in with emotion on every trip back to North Africa.

If the early indicators of British decolonisation in Kenya were the sole reason for their reluctant departure, those of French decolonisation in Algeria confirmed their hunch to distance themselves from the still-so-*blanche*. A post in the Congo would normally have tempted the two adventurers, but not with a child. So they resigned themselves to going back to square one. Once again, leaving everything behind them. Especially this land, my land of the *pieds-noirs*. Already trembling from being immersed in attacks, repression, assassinations, rivalries, war, and the blood. The blood on the incarnadined white, illuminated by the Mediterranean sun, resentment, and hatred. As the great empires of state tyranny crumbled despite their recalcitrant pretensions, Pierre-André and Suzanne were preparing to return to the working-class town, which they hoped would be less sleepy, to introduce their little Mireille to it...

6
The Return

The crossing with hundreds, soon to be hundreds of thousands, of other *pieds-noirs* was made by boat. Algeria-Marseille. Then the train. Finally came the station in this working-class town that was on the verge of making a name for itself, thanks to its watchmaking industry. André and Aline were on the platform. My grandmother took me in her arms, and I immediately felt at ease. She emanated that unalterable, unaltered serenity that I felt within her until her last breath. Even beyond that. I remember her soothing beauty at 89 years old in her coffin with her long hair and her smile. Never a rude word, never a malicious judgment, never the slightest grumble. Since I didn't have to endure the inflexible constraints of her ecclesiastical environment, I received only the quintessence of her faith. The one she had harmonised. Her permanent dialogue with God. Her trust. Her justice. Her bravery in enduring what I discovered years later on buying her her first swimming costume. A ball of flesh expelled from her vagina, after a prolapse of the womb. Like those bubbles of chewing gum we used to enjoy as kids, blowing them up in our mouths. She had been 34 when her son was born. Her uterus didn't survive what was a difficult delivery, and at a time of unemployment, she didn't have the means to treat it. This led to a providential excommunication from all sexual relations with André, seven years her junior. Ultimately, sexuality had fulfilled its role in conceiving a child, no doubt with the help of the Holy Spirit, as Mum said. The rest was sin. One day my mother asked her if she wasn't concerned about her husband's libido. She replied that "it" sorted itself out through natural channels. All the while, cuddling us with such sensual gentleness. Castrated sensuality; Eros beaten back right from the cradle. Yet her faith has permeated me. Especially her authentic humility. A very rare humility not once simulated nor even stimulated by any external factors. And anyway, even if their relationship was never associated with sexual passion, they still managed to hold onto a moving mutual tenderness for nearly 70 years.

Dad had no trouble finding a job. The five of us lived in a modest ground floor apartment, artistically decorated thanks to my grandfather's talents. He was a polisher in a watch factory where his talents took second place to productivity. Alas, his love for me intensified his obsession with bringing the entire family back to the church. He was simply terrified that those he held most dear would end up in Gehenna. His heart burst in the face of the nightmare of inevitable separation on the day of judgement. Just as bad, Suzanne had encouraged Pierre-André to join the masonic lodge, a means to get noticed and to network. For the whole colonial experience had made communication difficult in this psychologically charged city. When André learned where his son spent his Wednesday evenings, he couldn't help but say to his daughter-in-law: "You've brought the devil into our family!"

Being snatched up by the Prince of Darkness in

the dark of that polar winter rekindled in Suzanne the traumas she had managed to subdue under the tropical blazes. This set in motion a domino effect of nervous breakdowns. Aline suffered. André panicked. Pierre-André fretted, and Suzanne screamed. Enough to make the Prince of Darkness gloat!

Bluette, for her part, urged her daughter to dump the ones she called "the two old dears" and the "broke loser" still infatuated with Chopin. Especially since she had gone up in the world. In reality, into a rented garret room next to the attic in her brother's cabin. She was willing to welcome her, with me of course, because she loved me.

Her too…

So I was loved. But very early on, I could sense my lovers' discomforts. So, most of the photos of me from that time already reveal a worried face. Moving to a council estate eased the relationships, as everyone found their boundaries, the territorial ones at least. And it was there, far from the tropical bustle, that one night under a full moon, my parents decided to try for Loulou…

7

Loulou's Birth

According to a book of spells, the full moon lends itself to the conception of a boy.

A boy.

To Mum, this signified the traditional French "le choix du roi", the king's choice, a girl and a boy.

But for Dad, it was much more than that. Payback to the world at long last! A strong, athletic boy, an eminent musician, with the intelligence and work ethic to make him a great surgeon. Or a physicist, perhaps?

Thus, from the very second of his conception, Loulou had no choice but to become a prodigy. In other words, to patch up his parents' wounds. The vocation of so many adorable babies who were actually quite happy causing mischief with complete abandon.

Even so, Loulou became the king of the mischief-makers. A heart stealing baby with a permanent smile, an angelic imp. While his breech birth was an ordeal, he was nonetheless an accomplice in his mother's pranks until the end. Even though we found out that he'd been born with Trisomy 8, when it triggered myelodysplasia, and developed into an acute terminal leukaemia in the last years of his life. He was 64 years old. A life stigmatised by a cursed extra chromosome, at a time when medicine still lacked adequate means of detection. The spirit of science whose noble destiny is to dedicate itself to the relief of suffering, not out of some arrogant curiosity or, worse, a devotion to destruction.

Just a little extra chromosome that by chance cut short the freedom that was so important to his path to maturity...

When the diagnosis finally came, Laurent called me with his dry humour:

"I'm a mongol, but no one can tell!"

I then did some research on this extra chromosome. How it might show itself. I identified possible symptoms:

Slowness in behaviour that people were quick to associate with indifference or laziness.

A tall stature that made him an imposing man, although Loulou, despite a superior intelligence, was like a disorientated kid throughout his life.

Bone and joint abnormalities, particu-larly in the feet (very deep plantar creases), but also in the spine.

Risk of myelodysplasia (bone marrow diseases) and myeloid leukaemia (blood cancers).

And the one that destroyed his childlike spirit, as well as his father's ambitions: *urinary tract abnormalities.*

In fact, at 10 years old, he was still wetting his sheets and underwear. Many child psychiatrists who, under his mother's admiring winks, Loulou drove up the wall, declared him to be perfectly healthy.

Was it a former, buried violence, rekindled by frustration, that drove my father to "train" him?

Following a "reassuring" medical report,

Loulou found himself having to pull down his trousers at dinner times and display his underwear to the family. Any "negligence" was then punished brutally with blows from a belt: "Stop, Daddy, I'm begging you!"

Even today, I can't bear without flinching the sight of a man undoing his belt. Even though that was a time when kids got hit for every tiny thing. I, for my part, took my fair share, from Mum too. I don't think it really shocked us. Some neighbours or friends weren't much better off. We simply feared our parents and managed to get around the beatings by lying. Alas, Loulou's underwear didn't know how to lie.

So he was beaten.

Beaten and loved...

After each of these tortures, which sometimes left marks on his body, came affection. Hugs, gifts, the many sports that, with no expense or time spared, Dad played with him. Always present, never missing a single evening to rush home from work to be with his family. Sharing in his mother's silliness. Seaside camping holidays. Violin lessons. Movies, carousels, games. Picnics. Day trips. Every weekend a family weekend. A family radiating togetherness...

Was the romantic chaos that followed him later linked to his associating love with punishment? Around the age of thirteen, coached by an alcoholic high school teacher, he began to drink...

And it was Dad's turn to suffer in the face of this teenager whose new stature was now a protection against the abuse of his "training". Sleepless nights spent waiting for him to return or hunting for him in bars. That's on the days when his car hadn't been borrowed; started without a key thanks to a trick. The panic when he ran away with his best friend. The improvised hideout when he deserted from military service. And later, the debts he paid off for him after a suicide attempt...

Despite his shrewd ingenuity, an innate musical charisma, and athletic achievements that landed him on the Swiss volleyball team, Loulou was expelled from one school after another. It was thanks to Dad's determination that he earned a watchmaking diploma.

He brought back from his stay in Germany a beautiful young woman, Jutta, his first wife. Mum adopted her instantly, and she remained her favourite. As if she was sealing the reunion with this language that "Jutta spoke with the same melodious accent as my father". Alcohol eventually got the better of this love match...

Although she went on to rebuild her life, some 40 years later Jutta created a wedding album to "relive how much she had been in love".

Synchronicity of fate:

I was having lunch round at Jutta's and discovered this album, when Loulou's daughter Mireille called me to tell me that her father had decided against plunging back into the abyss of more chemotherapy. We collapsed in each other's arms. Then she told me:

"Laurent would never hurt a fly!"

Thank you, Jutta, for this tender testimony...

A few years after that first marriage, he ran into a New Zealander on a café terrace.

Her mother, Shirley, had gone through the ordeal of multiple sclerosis. Her father, Atholl, that of lung cancer. Judith was divorced and had just separated herself from the tenant she had been sharing her apartment with. Looking for a partner for her best friend, she approached this "handsome guy". They talked business, and she suggested that he come back a few days later when she would introduce him to a businesswoman. She returned alone. They spent the weekend in each other's arms, listening to Chopin. On Monday morning, when her boss asked her why she was daydreaming more than working, she replied: "I just met the man of my dreams…"

Married, she encouraged him to take advanced courses so as to become the manager of a large watch and jewellery store. She bore him two daughters. Alas, the handsome guy's psychological imbalance and his addiction dismantled his self-belief about a successful future in business. The separation was crucifying for both of them. He loved his two children, Mireille and Rebecca.

Another atonement for love…

When Judith was diagnosed with bone cancer, she returned to Auckland so that her sister could look after her daughters. She died shortly after, and Laurent struggled to repatriate them. A desperate attempt to mend the rifts, his own and theirs. He moved in with a sommelier he met in a bar, the mother of a boy who became the big brother. Blended family: Five members, a cat, alcohol, and... ignorance.

Perfidious ignorance.

Indifferent, imperturbable, narcissistic ignorance.

Ignoble ignorance, stripping away all compassion.

All that remained was self-destruction, one abyss after another, until he developed leukaemia and the "laziness" of no longer fighting. For what? The glimmer that in another world he didn't believe in, there would be love? The real deal, the love he'd been searching for his whole shitty life?

Fortunately, there were some almost joyful days. Business trips around the world, a position in the research lab of a renowned watchmaking firm with colleagues who had become partners in crime. Yes, little brother, right under the nose of that fucking chromosome, you've managed to have a great career! Bravo, my Loulou, bravo! Sharing love with his children. Discovering Africa. Asia. Cuba, although he was urgently repatriated from the latter, possibly an early warning sign. The closing rays of light in the lair of hell were when his daughter Mireille, during the last months of his life, held onto his hand…

In 2014, at the age of 90, Dad was hospitalised with multiple disorders. The palliative morphine Laurent had obtained from the doctor took several days to impact his still-strong heart. I was by his side day and night. In pieces. Powerless. Exhausted. The Hades of agony. On the last morning, Laurent accompanied me. Semi-conscious at that point, the old man was having hallucinations. Agitated, he constantly got up in bed, baring his teeth and shaking his fist. As if he were facing his old demons before what he was ultimately to describe as "a journey". It was then that his strong son, who never became a surgeon or a physicist, whispered to him:

"Relax, man, let yourself go…"

Then he went back to work, managing his pain as best he could.

I was left alone with my father, who, towards evening, was panting more and more. I took him in my arms:

"Aline is on her way to get you, don't be afraid!"

Those were the most atrocious days of my life.

A few months later, Laurent spat out his pain about it in expletives just like his mother:

"Life shat on him. Shat on him for ten years while he cared for his wife in solitude. Shat on him in the last months of his life. Shat on him before he died. And that pains me..."

A family radiating togetherness?

Or drifting hearts clinging to each other in a love undermined by evil? Malign evil sequestering the keys to knowledge, science, therapy, and forgiveness. But a family nonetheless, with the freedom to sin in choosing the wrong path. That sin of pride. That self-sufficient complacency that refuses to cry for help. That sordid pride that won't risk swapping its own brilliance for the compromise of a lifetime of mediocrity. Steering clear of too many aborted enthusiasms and too much productive hard work.

In 2015, after a stroke, Mum fearlessly wished to be allowed to join her Pierre-André. The one to whom she had said, not fussed about the gathering who had come, some plainly only out of social decency, to say their goodbyes:

"You know, Pierre, you were the only love of my life!"

"You too, my darling!"

In her last minutes, she tried to show me, with her face lit up, someone in the corner of her room:

"I see... I see..."

You could hardly speak anymore, my dear mother, and your eyes were already drifting into another world. But I know that he came looking for you, your great, great love. As for Laurent, he was deeply affected, for he adored his mother.

March 2016, a new, even more crushing labyrinth:

Leukaemia...

A faceless martyrdom. Hopes. Relapses. Journeys through darkness. Until that last grin. The one that both relieved the unbearable torture of seeing him disfigured in Sheol, but sank a dull dagger into my heart forever, despite life carrying on.

This is how I became the last of the four Favre-Bulles...

In fact, there could have been five of us. But Mum's third pregnancy, threatening her life, had to be terminated. The equation was simple: spare the mother of two children or the unborn baby! Not only did Dr. Kalbermatten save our mother, but he allowed the sharpshooter to express himself with no holds barred, so to speak, by tying his beloved's tubes. A procedure generously made available, as she didn't have the money for it. Suffice it to say that, when the same doctor was accused of enriching himself through abortions during the 1970s, Mum didn't go unnoticed among the defence witnesses. Thus, I owe my birth to the English abortionist's vacation in Mombasa, and I owe it to the Swiss abortionist that I was able to grow up with my lovely mother...

Our quartet was often envied, applauded, even feared. A provocative quartet, strengthened by a form of fusional love. Stars, especially in childhood, before the scars. Looking back, I feel that my existence, thanks to a *chance* diary clash, was marked by a kind of guilt. As if sometimes I had to justify breathing and disturbing others...

If marriage is often synonymous with neuroses that try to make compromises, so the child, too, is made to absorb those of his or her parents. But their strengths too. To Pierre-André and Suzanne I owe this transmission of never giving up. I realised this when I saw them, on the verge of retirement, lose their jobs during the watchmaking crisis of the 1980s. Deciding for a third time to leave everything behind, they went to the south of Spain. Lean years before retirement but also, at last, years of palm trees! Yet, as Dad confided to me:

"You quit your job and suddenly, you're nothing! Nobody anymore..."

Despite the palm trees, they went through those first months of exile depressed...

Then, Suzanne found a choir, which Pierre-André was quick to conduct for 15 years. Suzanne also hosted dance evenings with a piano bar and friends, as part of the *Cicadas*, a name she had chosen for the group. They brought out their classical repertoire on the piano too, playing four-handed every day or accompanying two Englishmen, former professional singers, in concerts. Mum learned Spanish again and organised long weekly outings with a walking group. Yes, the two eternal lovers had the guts to start all over again! A successful wager, as it was a time of sunshine despite the difficulties...

When I feel on the edge of an abyss, whatever it may be, I roll up my sleeves and say out loud Mum's life-saving phrase:

"Get off your ass, Maria... Well, what's left of it!"

Thank you, my dear parents, for that example of resilience...

8
Bluette's Blueprint

As a child, my grandmother Bluette stuffed me with food, because I was the chosen one of the family who received the privilege of her affection. Stuffed full with food, which delighted my sweet tooth and reinforced her sense of belonging. Stuffed full with her anxieties too. The main one being a paranoid obsession in the Sixties, left untreated. She was convinced that the Gestapo wanted her skin and she had included me in the whole plot. I took on my role within this psychodrama without realising its seriousness, or the scars it inflicted on my soul. I had lunch at her house every Friday. My bulimia savoured the set menu that didn't vary: veal sausage roasted in 200 grammes of butter into which was poured a tin of peas. Dessert: meringues, cream puffs, millefeuille.

Upon my departure, she would inspect the street. It was the hour when a giant of a neighbour, dressed in a long black leather coat and an equally black leather hat, would wait, one cigarette after another, for his black mastiff, as gigantic as he was, to deposit his waste on the pavement. This could last for quite some time. It was inconceivable that I should go out at that moment. To appease my impatience, I would receive the highlight of my meal: a tin of sweetened condensed milk that I savoured with a teaspoon, keeping an eye on the mastiff and our potential executioner.

While out walking, at the sight of the slightest suspect, she would drag me hastily into a stairwell. We would wait, cone of pepper in hand, for the suspect to move away. She would then harp on about never speaking to a stranger, because they could do me so much harm. The harm in question remaining as unnamed as it was unspeakable; I imagined for a long time that he would stick pins in my head...

Later, she was convinced that "they" came to the house while she was away. A balance wheel or spring that she used for her work as a watch technician would be found in a cup of water. She stuck stamps around her opened bottles of medicine so that "they" wouldn't poison her. One night, our father self-sacrificingly stayed up alone at her house. Having discovered nothing, he was accused of complicity…

She ended her life in this madness. In the depths of a slum with no bathroom, no toilet, and no heating. When the nights turned Siberian, she relieved herself in large buckets hidden under the bed, so she wouldn't have to go down to the toilets in the stairwell. Even though she had a good salary. Although she blew her earnings in top restaurants. It wasn't uncommon for her to visit three in a row. Or in buying new clothes, because she never did laundry in the only kitchen sink…

When she died of a heart attack, I was 14. I was the only one who mourned her. It must be said that she had played her part in sabotaging emotional ties. When Mother visited her, she would shout at her:

"No one can see past your nose!"

Dead, we hadn't been able to see her. The undertaker, a former admirer of Mum's, had said to us, eyeing her with delicate compassion:

"I can describe her to you: her face is blue and her eyes are swollen like two fists."

Did she commit suicide, as she had constantly threatened?

"I'm getting the hell out of here!"

Or was it simply her heart, stuffed with food, indigestion tablets, and Saridon, that had exploded? At the crematorium, her coffin seemed enormous. At the end of the ceremony, I saw her being lowered into the flames. I was shaken and found death abominable.

I often thought about it; it obsessed me.

I needed to know...

9
Death

Hence my plan to slip into the cold rooms of the crematorium pavillion to spy on death. As a general rule, funerals always departed from the final home with flower-covered processions. Or for a wealthy notable, the town band playing Chopin's funeral march. Such processions attracted me. I followed them. I tracked them. I spied on them. So it was mostly the lonelier ones who ended up at the pavillion.

My first visit was to an old woman behind a glass case. With the same features as all the dead who ultimately resemble each other. I went back several times, watching for a sign. Nothing. Nothing other than this placidity of colourless peel. One day, I even dragged my first flame there. A boy from a good family, very attentive. He radiated a natural kindness, while being a solid and balanced guy. Too much so for me, no doubt. He could cope with my macabre expeditions, but that didn't stop me from preferring competitors whose deviances would be more in keeping with my own...

As for death, it emerged as an adversary whose knots needed untying.

Among my loved ones, there were two radically opposing attitudes:

André's, terrorised perpetually by the Grim Reaper. He always spoke of him in a low voice, as if afraid of upsetting him. Whenever a friend or family member died of a heart attack, he would whisper:

"A beautiful death, he didn't feel a thing!"

As a child and teenager, I would have given anything to distract him from his nightmares. While it was he who was piling them up in my own soul. Even if that turned out to be the catalyst that sent me in search of encounters.

With Mum, it was the opposite. I've never met anyone so fearless in the face of death. She often mocked André:

"He's so scared, he'll end up shitting himself to death!"

Which is what happened...

As for her, she was eminently calm. As a young girl, as an adult, and as the deadline approached. One day, she suffered a kind of poisoning:

"I'm not scared, but swear to me you'll take care of Dad!"

Another time, at the home, she was taking a few steps with her walking frame, supported by a nursing assistant. She eyed her mockingly:

"I'll get through this, let me tell you!"

The nurse was embarrassed:

"Of course, Mrs. Favre-Bulle, of course..."

Mum burst into a laugh:

"I *will* get through this, 'cos I'll soon be on the other side!"

Finally, after a second stroke, helpless, she claimed the passport she needed to find her Pierre-André. I remember asking her:

"Mum, do you want to *leave?*"

Because I couldn't pronounce the fatal word.

She took leave to mean leaving the home where she was well cared for. So she shook her head.

I gathered all my strength and dared to say:

"Mum, do you want to die?"

She murmured, already radiant with the reunion:

"Yes, yes, yes!"

So she was spared non-stop therapy...

It was shortly after Bluette's death that my parents, influenced by a freemason friend, had begun their research into dreams. Dad had bought the collected works of Carl Gustav Jung, which they both absorbed, reminded that there was indeed another world. Other than that of their rebellious atheism or the prison of the family sect. A procession of novices from different fraternities was set in motion, and I watched enthusiastically as initiates from all walks of life filed past.

Surely there would be one who would eventually give me a clue...

10
Exaltations

Among those gurus from my childhood, there are three that I remember fondly:

We called him "Uncle Charles". A retired postman who lived in a village overlooking a Swiss lake. He had bequeathed half of his land to the Rosicrucian Society, on which he built them a temple. I was about 15 years old, and although I didn't attend the services, I admired this man whose kindness and simplicity touched me. Rosicrucians ascend the ladder of cosmic wisdom by degrees of initiation and believe in reincarnation. For me, this evoked a more acceptable negotiation with death. Because the soul was abandoning this colourless peel to take on another, it took with it its karma – that is, its actions and thoughts, which influenced the destiny of its next reincarnation. Uncle Charles, who also had healing gifts, turned out to be a reincarnation of Paracelsus.

Having myself practiced the daily mirror ritual, to the rhythm of Albinoni's *Adagio*, I ended up one evening, by dint of staring at the hypnotic point, encountering an Egyptian woman wearing a pharaonic tiara. Obviously, my underlying megalomania did not lead me to the vision of a slave or a servant. Uncle Charles, on the other hand, was supposed to detach from himself frequently. Specifically, he would leave his body to join his Tibetan master in the celestial spheres. I never succeeded in detaching from myself, a crucial step that, as a manoeuvre, only death had mastered. But I indulged in a frenzied enthusiasm for it. My poor Laurent had felt an explosion in his head during his mirror session, which he abandoned forever, along with any form of belief. So, when, at the zenith of my delirium, I ordered the wind to calm down, he quipped: "There goes the Messiah!"

I would skip class to hitchhike to Uncle Charles's. He was always the same. Sitting lotus-style on his sofa. Taking my questions with innate candour. Mostly, I had to be content with the enigmatic light of his immense blue eyes. In the middle of a very round face. Under a very round bald head. Overlooking a very round belly. He recommended readings, including those of Lobsang Rampa, a British man born in Tibet who became a medical Lama. He never asked me for a penny, nor did he try to draw me to him. Which, in hindsight, excludes him from the humbly seductive and sweetly avaricious seigneury of spiritualists. He offered me potions of his own concoction for a painful bump on my heel, and the treatment worked well. One day, I expressed a wish to become a Dove, a virgin integrated into Rosicrucian ceremonies. I imagined myself as a sublime vestal virgin between the columns of the temple. A week before, a new initiate, very popular at home, who came from a more secretive and seemingly wiser fraternity, declared the initiation ritual "dangerous." I renounced it. To be honest, I was as bemused as I was excited...

It was the Vietnam War, against which I and my friends were demonstrating, that drew me to one of the apostles of non-violence of the Seventies, Lanza del Vasto:

He was giving a lecture in our town. He arrived barefoot, draped in a white tunic. His hair was just as white as his beard and he had thick eyebrows. His face was majestic, swarthy. His gaze was as dense as it was black. A prophetic appearance crafted with skill and an intense scent of the Orient. His concept of us all returning to a shared rural agriculture, to just meet basic needs without anything left over, didn't appeal to me. On the other hand, his violent passion for active non-violence, based on his concept of being neither exploitative nor exploited, ignited my increasingly social justice-oriented impulses. During his talk, the term "sin" led me to ask him the question that was beginning to intrigue me:

"What *is* sin?"

I didn't get an answer, which only heightened my curiosity. I remember the murmur of the elderly ladies in the room. Perhaps because of my bleached hair down to my backside, barely concealed by my miniskirt.

At the end of the evening, legs bare and head

held high, my starlet face sparkling, I lined up to greet him. He took my hand solicitously:

"You will study psychology!"

He had the aura of a prophet…

A year after his death, *chance* would have it that I participated in an Orthodox chanting workshop. Welcomed by a *L'Arche* community that he had founded, modelled on Gandhi's ashrams. So in the evenings, I attended their meetings…

Increasingly knotted up in the mysteries of sin, I made a point of devoting myself to other readings, such as those of Krishnamurti, Arnaud Desjardins, Buddhist or Chinese wisdom, and the essential Hermann Hesse. Especially the work of Karlfried Graf Dürckheim, a friend of Jung, Paul Klee and Rilke. His mission to bring back to us the Zen he had deepened in Japan, with an occidental slant, seemed to crown my intuitions. As did his teaching about joining action to word by cementing them together through a precise routine, as he himself had done with archery. Finally, his invitation to pursue the numinous, summoning into consciousness another reality, where the small ego would dissolve into the great divine Ego.

So I went, legs still bare and head still held high, to the Black Forest, to Todtmoos. Another splendid old man, with blue eyes that were almost haughty and the stature of the noble man he was. A unstabling encounter, if only because of his concentration and the energy of his presence. He gave me a demonstration on mastering energies, actually. He formed a circle with his thumb and index finger, barely touching. He claimed that by concentrating all his energy on it, no one would be able to separate his two fingers. I clung to it with all my might, without success. This display awakened my awareness of energies as a gift. Lose them or multiply them tenfold? But I didn't learn any more about sin…

Little by little, I abandoned my contemplative ambitions to take refuge in atheism. Besides, how could any being, even a slightly superior one, allow millions of innocent people to be roasted in ovens and children to be grilled with napalm bombs? That is how I became less and less excited and… more and more lost…

11

Because He Could Do Me So Much Harm

My grandmother Bluette's repeated warning could have had a disastrous real-life echo:

The first time was before my maths oral. One Sunday, my friend Monique and I had arranged a revision picnic. Hitchhiking! A man in his forties picked us up and drove us to the Doubs region. In the middle of the countryside, we asked him to stop at the side of a secluded road. Opposite was a steep field, which we duly climbed before settling ourselves down at the edge of the forest. Not a farm, not a soul in sight. Absolute calm. Ideal for studying.

After lunch, we took out our lesson notes. All of a sudden, we could make out the car that had brought us there. It was driving very slowly along the country road. Same driver, this time accompanied by two friends. The car parked just below the field where he had dropped us off. The three men stayed inside. All three of them were watching us, cigarettes dangling from their lips. We realised they weren't there to help with our maths! Panicked, we did our best to assess the situation. Mathematically speaking, we had zero chance of escaping them. Two young females, hidden from sight in the wilderness. No mobile phones yet! All that remained for us was a *chance* nudge in the right direction.

Although there had been no cars passing by since we arrived, we spotted one in the distance. We rushed to it, and at that moment the driver started his engine. We raced, yelling and gesticulating so the car would see us. It stopped while the three troublemakers sped off. A couple with a child took us back to the town.

This *chance* wink ensured that my suffering was confined to the maths oral...

Another wink came some 15 years later. In my thirties, legs still bare in white ankle boots, head still held high. I was pacing back and forth at the

Gare de Lyon in Paris, elegantly dressed. I remember how I looked, resplendent in my suit with its flared, wavy skirt. My white handbag. My white fitted blouse, and my waist-length hair, this time a reddish-brown.

The TGV bringing my husband from Marseille was very late. I meandered about, alert and perfumed. Yves Saint Laurent's *Rive Gauche*. Suddenly, a guy came up behind me and deftly slid his hand under my skirt. He pinched my backside with a ferocity before creeping away.

Shaken, I took refuge in the nearest café. As soon as I had sat down, two hellhounds entered and immediately headed over to me: "Madame, you were sexually assaulted, and you're not the only one. Can you come with us to testify?"

Another one of those flashes of *chance*, once again turning everything on its head. Rather than play the offended bourgeoise, I shouted without even realising:

"Leave me alone, I don't want to testify against anything at all!"

They took off like a pair of skyrockets, and it was under the barely disturbed gaze of the other customers that I was then able to order my tea.

Since then, every time I think back to these two misadventures, I shudder with both fear and gratitude. Others haven't had this *good fortune*, at the right time. To the nearest second. *Chance?* The kind that just manages to stop everything from capsizing into horror…

12

The Joys of *Destiny!*

Another of these *chance* occurrences happened in Italy. In the sea. I was about 15 years old. An unusual storm with raging waves was breaking against the seawall at the beach where the four of us were holidaying. I went swimming very close to this breakwater. I was in high spirits. I swam underwater as I often do. Suddenly, I was sucked into a passage on the other side of the seawall. Thrown onto the rocks, I grabbed onto them to pull myself up, but the ebb tide pulled me away again. These successive rises and falls quickly exhausted me. Such power! Such helplessness! Instinctive screaming. As *chance* would have it, a young German couple was "playing around" on the rocks. Holding on tight, the man managed to pull me out of the raging waves. They were alone on that seawall, as in the Garden of Eden...

Chance was again at play, that August evening when I took a flight in a teaching colleague's old Piper, over my beloved high school. A cheerful daredevil 365 days a year. He had sat me in the front, my hair and nostrils facing the zephyrs. As he filled the tank, he was singing one of his favourite songs.

While taking off, I shouted at him that there was a smell of fuel:

"No worries, we'll soon be flying over the school!"

Right before I could admire the place I called "my home" from sky level, he placed both hands heavily on my shoulders:

"Don't panic, we're going to make a good landing!"

Except there wasn't a single airfield in sight?

Then the daredevil, without breaking anything other than a few ears of wheat and my backside, actually managed to make a good landing in a field:

"But? What happened?"

He had forgotten to close the fuel tank! In the

photos taken by another colleague, it can still be seen on the wing, just before take-off...

I then rushed into those ears of wheat that were still standing. I had reached a turning point as I looked up at the sky. And the atheist in me cried out:

"Thank you, God, thank you for life!"

13

The Masters ... of School

"Hold out your hand to him and ask for his forgiveness!"

The exhortation from a soporific spinster, to force us to resolve our conflicts. This led a few years later to Laurent being paired up with the other Laurent in his class. The two Laurents, having refused to forgive each other after a fight and having been sent to the headmaster, quickly became complicit buddies. Incompatibility with this moralist, as well as our recent house move, meant I had to leave behind my beloved first teacher. The one who, along with Mum, encouraged me to write from a very early age.

Another lonely old maid cast a shadow over primary school for me, discouraging me at the slightest opportunity, because I had deemed RE to be less important than science.

Yes, it was still the time when teachers didn't marry...

My most poignant memory from high school remains my old Latin teacher, John Nussbaum. He adored me:

"If you didn't exist, we'd have to invent you!"

Amused by the hippie patterns I drew on my legs and by my hair adorned with equally hippie flowers. A fanatic for the Roman language, culture, and history. A colossus over seven decades old, with a Herculean voice, who led the way on school trips, like Julius Caesar before his troops. With his handkerchief tied at the four corners as a hat. Not only did his introductions to grammar make it easier for me to study any other foreign language, but I remember every one of his historical anecdotes. Especially the one about Hannibal crossing the Alps with his elephants or those about Caesar. I particularly loved it when he mimed the scene for us of the Egyptians presenting Caesar with the head of his enemy, Pompey, whom they had decapitated to please him:

"And before this white head, Caesar wept..."

I was so captivated that I declared that if I ever had a son, he would be named Caesar Hannibal. It was John's approach that inspired me when I became a high school French teacher in German-speaking Switzerland. Not just to wing the language, but to bring the country where he was born to life, its flaws, its moments of light, its soul. John, a Christian who only imposed his faith by example, managed to be so close to us despite all the while remaining an antique figure. Such nobility!

At the high school in La Chaux-de-Fonds where I taught, there were, of course, atheists. With its leftish, if not leftist, tradition.

Among them was the writer Yves Velan, winner of the Grand Prix C. F. Ramuz. He arrived in La Chaux-de-Fonds *by chance*, a "happening" town to which he would remain attached until his death. He immediately enjoyed a certain prestige there, having been banned from teaching in the Canton of Vaud because of his involvement in the Swiss Communist Party. A party that, like so many others, he would leave at the beginning of the Sixties. As a teenager, disgusted that my grandfather had worked for a pittance, while his boss never held off from flaunting his wealth, I had no trouble in getting intoxicated by this character. With his raincoat collar always turned up, his wry humour and his dark eyes as fiery as they were inflaming. I rushed to buy his first novel *Je* published by Seuil in 1959. I had trouble getting involved in the interior monologue of the Vaudois pastor, even if his doubts, his questions, his feelings of guilt echoed my grandfather's anxieties. I also remember our secret giggles upon reading the passage about the pastor going to a prostitute. As for its backdrop of the social struggles in French-speaking Switzerland, it brought me closer to my new impulse, POP, the Popular Workers' Party (the *Parti Ouvrier Populaire*). If my blossoming brain wasn't up to carrying its own novel, I trembled like the others when Velan entered the classroom. More captivated, in fact, by his gaze than by his words! I remember my first essay: "The Sound of Rain". Intent on instilling within us the rigour he imposed on himself, he had crossed out the first five pages of my lyrical description of the forest. *Off-topic, a flood of superfluous words.*

His jokes too, all kinds of them:

"What did Christopher Columbus bring back from America?"

We replied:

"Potatoes, tobacco?..."

A Velanish grin:

"Syphilis!"

Like John Nussbaum, Velan was one of those educators who brought a vibrancy to their teaching. He, moreover, was sensitive. So, what was instilled above all was transmission through emotion. It was he who introduced me to writing, and thanks to him, I was also able to play in the schools' theatre troupe directed by another example, Edgar Tripet.

If Velan was a tormented soul, Tripet was the very model of smiling equilibrium. Whatever the subject, he presented it with the same serene voice. Historian, writer until his last breath in 2020, man of culture, art, cinema, theatre, director of the Lycée Blaise Cendrars in La Chaux-de-Fonds, above all Edgar inspired me with his creative power of tolerance. His tolerance.

His youth had been mutilated by his father's suicide, and by a mother who paid him little attention and entrusted him to the care of his grandparents. But he had been illumined too, by teachers like Jean-Paul Zimmermann, the rebellious literature professor. With Tripet, we experienced May '68, which he used to instil in us a taste of liberation. Liberation from the shackles of a rigid world, without quite toppling human responsibility. A sublime and immutable schooling. Thank you, Edgar!

What remains of that era?

"The worst thing is bigotry!" Mum would proclaim constantly. I second that, I second that again, and I will always second that!

John Nussbaum, the legacy of ancient times. A less subjective, more global perception of history and the present. The living love of a dead language that takes on life and whose structures structure the mind. A counterweight to our brilliant computerisation? Because John was a soul. A heart. A passion. For transmitting ideas…

For Yves Velan, it was about constant questioning, including self-questioning, in order to escape any form of totalitarian control over thought. As for writing, far from just being about vomiting out words, it requires a communion through its own distilling questioning.

For Edgar Tripet, it was about an unrestricted openness because man is capable of maturing, of creating, and we must trust in him.

My inestimable gratitude to these schoolmasters. To these masters, period…

14
First Stirrings for Artistic and Historical Literature

The ones that enriched my daydreams.

My parents took turns in reading our bedtime stories to us; I cried so much at the death of Gribouille (Countess of Ségur).

Laurent and I would shiver listening to little 45s of Perrault's tales on repeat. And from the stories I invented lying in bed on Sunday mornings, too, while my parents were busy enjoying each other. And those I imagined when we were in the sea with our holiday friends.

Aline and André would tell me biblical stories. The frail young David who defeated Goliath thanks to his inspired ingenuity was my favourite.

I owe my first tears in front of the big screen to Jean Gabin. I was about ten years old, and I can still see old Jean Valjean extinguished in front of Cosette's doll. Abandoned in poverty.

Initiation into the tremors of love:

Belmondo and especially Lino Ventura, whose ardently reassuring gaze still makes my white hair stand on end.

Jeanne Moreau captivated me. Especially after watching *Mata Hari*, a film I went to see with my father. I was 15, and I needed to be 18. So, Mum had fashioned my hair into a grown-up bun and smeared my lips with a generous layer of lipstick so I could walk tall in front of the policeman who was making sure the age limit was respected. Nothing too disconcerting, except for her bare breasts dancing beneath her veils. Breasts that on the posters were camouflaged by a white strip. No different from any cabaret window. About ten years later, when women were burning bras, I catapulted mine into the trash to give myself a bosomy thrill! Looking back, however, it seems to me that I was immersed in a form of modest exhibitionism. More of a return to nature. An almost naive naturalness. Playful, provocateur of peace. Even if my liberated breasts, the flowers drawn on my legs, and those in my hair, served only to add colour to the entrenched family neuroses.

At the high school film club, the film that shook me was Alain Resnais' Holocaust film, *Nuit et Brouillard*. ('Night and Fog'). We didn't have social media. Assassinations came in live. Visual overload. So these kinds of films fuelled our debates for weeks. And already with *Nuit et Brouillard*, we were asking ourselves the question:

"Could this happen again?"...

As for the music:

My Elvis, the most sensual, the most heavenly voice!

Of course, I mourned for Brel and Barbara...

My very first book as a child was James Shaw's *Bela, fille de la jungle* ('Jungle Girl'). I especially remember the ending, when her lifelong friend Budi finds his princess. It was fabulous to dream back up the entire storyline, which I did endlessly. What a catalyst for the imagination!

I also enjoyed the legends of ancient Egypt and, in high school, the ending of Flaubert's *Salammbô* made me shudder.

I was very moved during my baccalaureate exams by that passage in Camus' *La Peste* ('The Plague') when Tarrou and Rieux bathe in communion in the heart of hell...

And then there were current events. The kind that engraved themselves on me because humanity was revealed in all its goodness or abomination. Information, as well as the disinformation, was medieval compared with today. It was still possible to weave one's fantasies around a character and concoct one's own hero.

In 1961, the atrocious assassination of Patrice Lumumba, the first prime minister of the Republic of the Congo, was discussed at every family meal. No doubt because Pierre-André and Suzanne would have gone to Congo if the abortionist hadn't been sunbathing on the beaches of Mombasa.

A year later, on July 5th, I learned that my homeland of Algeria had got its independence...

That same year, 1962, in October, I realised, at the tender age of 12, that an atomic war could destroy everything. The Cuban Missile Crisis and John Fitzgerald Kennedy's ultimatum to Nikita

Khrushchev, despite Mum thinking the latter had a cute face!

On January 22, 1963, I was eating as usual at my grandmother Bluette's house. For dessert, before I devoured my pastries, she threw me the day's newspaper, *L'Impartial,* which the whole town consulted, mainly for the death notices:

"Look at that backstabbing face!"

The backstabbing face belonged to the German, Adenauer. Being embraced by my hero, General de Gaulle. The one we nicknamed "our great Charles!" I never missed a single one of his speeches. I truly felt sincere grief when Pompidou announced, on November 9, 1970:

"France is a widow!"

As late as 1963, the cover photo of the same *L'Impartial* showed the car from Dallas with Jacqueline Kennedy on top of her assassinated husband. We had just got a television, and the whole family sobbed when little three-year-old John saluted in front of his father's coffin. I was six years old when the Russians attacked Hungary. We hung white cloths out of the window to signal to the Red Cross that parcels were available. I was

15 when the second Vietnam War began. I was 17 when the six-day war in the Middle East began. I was 18 when Russian tanks entered Prague. We were having lunch at the supermarket restaurant with Mum, and the radio announced the invasion. These are the events that left the biggest impression on me. Along with De Gaulle, two opposing figures are etched into my admiration: the sublime grandmother Golda Meir and Anwar El Sadat. When the latter was assassinated, I was at home with the flu. One of my students, her name was Suzanne, to whom I had lent his autobiography, called me to tell me of his death. We consoled each other...

Finally, in 1970, the first plane hijackings, when one of our Swissair planes was hijacked (along with others) in the Zarqa desert in Jordan by the PFLP, demanding the release of Palestinian detainees in Kloten and Munich. I had just had my maiden flight to London. Hastily boarded at the last minute, without the slightest baggage or security check...

I won't retrace the history of the *Trente Glorieuses*. Injustice, barbarity, and fanaticism were no strangers to them either. However, we had the fabulous opportunity at that time to establish our group therapy sessions. Gathered daily in the same brasserie for heated discussions, for us this was an opportunity to speak freely. A privilege we were unaware of, especially when compared to the anonymity of anti-social networks nowadays...

There were also some truly glorious technical leaps. In 1961, the first man orbited the earth. No one imagined that one day, the human race would waste billions in space to fuel its pride, while famine continued to lay populations to waste! On July 20, 1969, celestial bodies welcomed the American spacecraft live on television around the world. In 1967, Professor Barnard successfully performed his first heart transplant...

Even at the end of the Glorieuses, during the first oil crisis of 1973, we wanted to continue working. For a more equitable, more developed world, filled with more madness. But madness puffed up with hope. At the end of 2024, as the white heat of war rages on, I don't know if the future is darker than it was for little Suzanne in her rathole. If the tears of an unemployed person are more bitter than those shed by André. If Ukrainian fighters, or victims of the October 7th attack, or the children of Gaza, deserve more stars on the scale of horror than *Nuit et Brouillard* or are more martyred than those of Vietnam. The suffering caused by human passions is not new. I mean, one of our first ancestors, Cain, had murdered his own brother in a fit of jealousy. So, along with so many others, and as preached by all the great philosophies, I remain convinced that it is in the human heart that selfishness, presumption, and envy must be hunted down. Teaching, especially about history, aside. Alas, this can't be done with one or two impatient clicks...

15
Childhood

A cockerel. My earliest memory. Too young to grasp that James had never left her heart, I was leaving the cemetery with my grandmother. I ventured into a farmyard. My grandmother Bluette, who was already turning crushing the bees that were gathering nectar along the road into an unfortunate habit, had fallen again. Broken her arm. She was in pain and holding it against her with her good hand. A cockerel charged at me to chase me away. Bluette rushed forward and kicked it back. I was more frightened than harmed, but still I see her, wincing in pain to protect her granddaughter.

"Get down and above all, keep quiet!"

Mum was plotting her revenge against the landlord who was renting us an apartment in one of the oldest buildings in La Chaux-de-Fonds. Another bigot, a church elder. He had filed a complaint of indecency against Mum because she had such severe back pain that she would put on her bikini at the slightest ray of sunshine in the garden. Her plan was to wait for the old bigot to come out and to fire several shots from the window with a cap gun. How delightful it was to play cowboys with our mother, who was undoubtedly the most excited of the three of us. The scheme worked, except that we kids couldn't hold back our bursts of laughter when the bigot jumped like a frightened rabbit. Mum, you were so lively, so funny, so cheeky, to make the comment you were so chuffed with...

"You're costing us a lot of money!"

A mug shot of André during a military parade in Lausanne. I supported his protest, especially after learning that in 1936, during demonstrations by the poor and neglected masses of the Swiss Confederation, he had charged onto an army horse to stop the procession come to restore order. Yet, he undertook his four-month military training, then all the refresher courses. True to his Christian commitment not to kill, he joined the stretcher-bearers. More than ever, I honour this attitude of "imposing" one's convictions while respecting democracy. Nevertheless, the Favre-Bulle family was anti-militaristic. As children, we saw our father leave every year for the military refresher courses. Though we were intrigued by the rifle and cartridges that, like all Swiss, he kept in the attic, one winter day our enthusiasm was cut short. Having been impatient for his return, we rushed into the garden: "Don't touch me, I stink, I haven't washed in three weeks!"

Later, during his military service training, Laurent wanted medical exemption, perhaps linked to the genetic disorder he suffered from. After several punishments, he deserted. Dad enlisted the support of his friend, a sympathetic rebel who hid him in his cabin before arranging a psychiatric assessment to legally free him from that chore. For my part, legs still bare and head still held high, I displayed my support for conscientious objectors. The latter were still imprisoned during their military service. Some were allowed out to work, only to go back to prison to sleep. Our heroes in the middle of the Vietnam War...

Over the years, I changed. Firstly, because several of my students had served in the army, then returned to take their baccalaureate. All of them had been transformed for the better. And then I gradually accepted that the ability to defend oneself was a necessary evil. While remaining, like so many Swiss people today, almost ontologically attached to our neutrality, regardless of the conflict. This has often allowed us to host peace summits worthy of the name...

"*The sea*, Mimi, Loulou, the sea!"

Nirvana before our very eyes and three weeks in swimsuits. Campsites at that time were poorly equipped. The smelly Turkish toilets, the inadequate showers, the scarce water. But the sea and the sun made up for everything we lacked. We came home burnt to the bone, our backs charred with rivers of salt running down them. The ritual of the immaculate underwear was effectively eliminated. Pure bliss! A basic diet, but always fruits, vegetables, *Laughing Cow* cheese, and condensed milk. Dad taught us to swim, dive, and play table tennis, and Mum let us explore freely or spend hours in the waves. We weren't rich, but we were privileged...

Our car, thanks to a budget managed to the nearest cent, was our goddess. I remember that blue Dauphine we went to pick up as a family. Dad paid one thousand-franc note after another for it because, in the Favre-Bulle household, there was a principle: never get into debt, so you can hold onto your freedom!

When Laurent started school, Mum, who had taken secretarial and English classes relentlessly, landed a job as a secretary. We would then have afternoon tea at Grandma Aline's house, before heading out with two neighbouring boys. The eldest of the four, I took the lead in this small male troupe, marking the start of a period of mischief, adventure, and a true conquest of the streets. It was all part of it: the impromptu choir to go sing for the elderly people who spoiled us, despite our mitigated performances; the bones for the dog that we begged the butcher for, which we roasted in the forest before gnawing at them; the expeditions in pursuit of treasure or bandits. One day, we stole the bottle of liqueur from Dad's bar leaving the four of us dead drunk on the pavement. Hygiene was completely lacking: we picked up chewing gum spat out on the road, and later, old cigarette butts for our first puffs of cigarettes. I retain from those years a feeling of light-heartedness and insouciance...

And studying?

Neither Laurent nor I were tryhards, despite our parents' obsession with seeing us excel. Rehashed through harsh remarks when we showed our poor results:

"All you're good for is cleaning the station toilets!"

Or again:

"When you have nothing to say, shut up!"

Laurent, who was a regular offender when it came to indiscipline, was nevertheless honoured in primary school by an old teacher who had a weakness for unruly children. For two years he finished like a superhero with a grade of 6 out of 6 in all subjects. Alas, the teachers that followed had other expectations and other methods...

As for me, and this continued until my

baccalaureate, I worked on French because I loved writing. History fascinated me, and as for the rest, it depended on the fluency of the teacher's style. Except for maths, which was always torture from the first to the last calculation...

At around 16, I wanted to stop my studies. My father hired me during the summer break to check the water resistance of the stopwatches at the company where he worked. A very efficacious vaccination that quickly brought me back to school. So that I could buy myself clothes, I was also "invited" to sell shoes on Wednesday and Saturday afternoons. Hours spent with my nose in shoes finally convinced me that parental recommendations had some basis in fact.

As athletes, we were spoiled by our parents who went without so as to invest in us. The same was true of culture and, very early on, we were dragged to museums. Rome, Florence, Paris. Paris enchanted me. I remember having our first meal there in a self-service restaurant. Drawn in by the menus scrolling before my ever-appreciative lips. Our parents also introduced us to their beloved classical music. Piano, violin, and guitar lessons.

Fruitful for the extremely gifted Laurent. In vain for me, who listened more than played. Pierre-André and Suzanne, despite their own bruises, strove to offer us everything they had been deprived of.

We were incapable of realising their sacrifices, too battered by their exclusivity and their barely healed scars. Having to face everything that, in their eyes, distracted them from the sacred quartet they had built with their love. Nowadays, it's much easier to get therapy before or during the arrival of children, which seems to me the most priceless jewel we can offer them...

16

Sex

Anatomically speaking, we were *au fait* with it all from early childhood. At home, we walked around "in the buff" as Mum said. We washed daily, one after the other, in the same bathtub because there wasn't enough hot water for four baths. When Suzanne suffered unbearable back pain, that rendered her bedridden or forced her to work all twisted up, a doctor recommended naturism. By the time we were teenagers, we had seen more genitals than all our peers combined, even the most liberated of them! Nevertheless, when it came to more elaborate insights, we were hardly advanced: "The daddy puts a small seed in the mummy's womb to make a baby!" However, we were suddenly and dramatically confronted with sodomy.

One day, our neighbour's son, whose stepfather was an alcoholic, spun me around and pinned me against the fence, pressing me against his dick. Overweight and with a glass eye, he terrified me. As Mum was about to bare her claws, we heard shouts from their apartment:

"Stop fucking that kid, you shithead!"

Then screams:

"Call the police!"

Which was done.

The "shithead" was arrested because, for good measure, he had just committed a major theft. The fat kid with the glass eye was separated for good from his abuser. And my parents decided to look for a more expensive rental with less scary tenants.

The event choked me up. I had suspicions that Bluette's *do me so much harm* wasn't just about having pins stuck in my head. A kid who was the same age as me, having his anus torn open in front of his own mother. What have you become, obese martyr? Atrociously torn apart by life, you who had mimed out with me what you yourself were going through? Have you managed to put yourself back together? To straighten yourself up on seeing, with your one eye, a little light?

Mum, for her part, seized on this trauma to warn us that an anus could be coveted by a nasty guy who would:

"Stick his cock in it!"

Although a few years later, the rebel would become good friends with her teaching colleague, a well-known homosexual, who met her in the café to confide his erotic dreams to her.

Caught up in her contradictions, she strove to protect our childhood in an almost bucolic way. Every time an insect or a toad mated on our path, she revealed to us that they were making love. But when Laurent, as a teenager, toured Europe with the Swiss volleyball team, Suzanne bought him condoms so he wouldn't catch an STD, or, in her words: "So he doesn't leave a poor fatherless boy in Greece or anywhere else!"

From the moment I got my first period, she confided in me that the most precious treasure was a small patch of skin at the entrance to my vagina, which had to be reserved for the man in my life, just as she had done for Dad. As for pleasure, the enjoyment linked to these organs which were created like any other, *that* belonged to our secret garden. We would find our ecstasy as they had so perfectly found theirs!

A time when erotic books were almost impossible to find, films in which you watched more than a kiss were censored for those under 18, and racy magazines only revealed breasts we knew by heart. It was reading Henry Miller's *Sexus* in secret that expanded my understanding through some very crude pornography. However, when I stayed out one summer evening, shortly after my twenties, Mum was quick to take me to our gynaecologist who prescribed me my first contraceptive pill.

Beyond that, Mum sometimes went against her father's advice, allowing me to parade around, as sexily as possible. Miniskirts, tank tops without a bra, or shorts with thigh-high leather boots. Because fashion, in its turn, was staking its claim to the May '68 liberation. Mum juggled between sparing me from the restrictive rules that she deemed bigoted and extolling the virtues of sexual modesty. Gifted with crafting, she made me an entire wardrobe out of cheap scraps of fabric, patterns, and her sewing machine. She also knitted our sweaters and Dad's. In taking such care with my outfits, I think she was instinctively taking revenge on the "old pigs" by watching them drool over my haughty provocations. But as for pleasure, I had to muddle through that myself. I'd felt that solo sexual activity was forbidden ever since I'd been punished violently by my grandmother Bluette when she caught me, as a child, caressing myself with my soft toy rabbit. From then on, her same question kept cropping up: "You won't be so naughty anymore, promise?" Promises never kept, and I regretted that what felt so good was so ugly...

I was stuck between several worlds. Suzanne's internal clashes that pushed me into overstepping the mark, Pierre-André's conservative outlook, Bluette's nightmares, Aline's silence, and André's frustrations. In a Switzerland where women only obtained the right to vote in 1971, I nevertheless managed out of those conflicting demands to navigate a path that brought me exaltation and reverie. Confident that this bustling world was within reach of my bare legs, my head held high, and my starlet's features...

17
The Lovers

Mum, secure in her family quartet, raised us as if we would never be separated. I even suspect she wouldn't have been shocked if I had become, like those ancient pharaohs she held dear, my brother's wife. Yet, often overwhelmed by the chaos in Laurent's room, she would say to him:

"I hope you find a woman who'll make you suffer!"

Without realising that her uncontrolled words destabilised our souls. While she defended us like a lioness against everything, everyone, and all, she never knew how to control her language.

While I felt admiring affection for my father, I don't think I carried the Oedipus complex around for long. Laurent, on the other hand, had practically transferred his love for his mother to his sister. I only realised it when one of my boyfriends, who came to our house for tea, received nothing but jokes bordering on aggression. Yet, he was the first to experience true love.

He must have been 16 years old. A face like an archangel, long, slightly curly hair, endless black eyelashes, and an athlete's body. In Yugoslavia, on a naturist paradise island where we were spending our vacations, he met a young French girl, a year his junior. Her father was a doctor. A bourgeois family who worshipped their only daughter like a divinity. Lovely blue eyes, thick ash-coloured hair, a model's body, and a small, upturned nose that gave her an aura of innocence. The two kids fell in love. During dance parties, he would hold her in a reverent embrace, holding her hand in his, against his chest, as if to keep her forever. Laughter, swimming, walks, carefree fun, and promises. They never left each other. On the day of departure, at dawn, we were in the car for a 950km journey. It was raining. The princess's father accompanied her to say goodbye. I never again saw Laurent look at a woman with such intensity. Not a word during the entire return trip.

The following year, they met again, passionately this time. And the third and final year, tumultuously. The princess started to reveal a slight disdain. But Laurent, the star of the campsite's volleyball team, was spoiled for choice. An adorable girl from Zurich offered to console him. Her Gallic Majesty changed her mind, goaded by her rival, who spent the rest of her holiday in tears.

As for the two lovers, it was madness. The drunken parties, the nights when I found myself in our little tent sleeping next to a half-drunk stranger who had lent his roof to the terrible lovers. This time the promises intensified to the point that the parents decided to visit us in Switzerland.

It was shortly before Pierre-André and Suzanne built a new house in the Jura countryside. We were still living in a four-room apartment, comfortable yes, but not enough to make Laurent a sufficiently wealthy match. The visit was brief and uneventful, except for the two lovers. Laurent remained secretive, but I felt that tragedy was approaching.

One day he took his dad's car to go to the other end of France. In the middle of the night, the doctor surprised them in the same bed. Laurent explained to him that he hadn't travelled so far just to sleep with his daughter, but that he loved her and wanted to spend his life with her. I heard through snippets of caught words that she was expecting a child. Eventually, the father arranged for an abortion. The breakup followed. Laurent sank into even more alcoholism, and the beautiful woman married a Parisian who fathered a son with her before abusing her. She divorced. A few years later, while visiting Switzerland, her parents couldn't help but sigh in the garden of the Juran villa: "How wonderful this place would have been for our grandchild!" But by then, the scalded suitor had just married his first wife. It just goes to show that sometimes happiness is only missed through a late start in building a few, forest-facing, concrete walls...

Decades later, during one of his many breaks from his last partner, I found Loulou in tears in his car, having finally phoned the love of his life:

"She remembers my beautiful arched feet!"

The only time I saw him cry over a woman...

"Never depend on a man, even the best!"

For my part, I was never burdened by my parents' financial pretensions. Quite the opposite! My mother, an accomplice in my extravagant femininity, pushed me to study and be independent. This influenced me so much that I always found any wealthy suitor a bit suspicious. Thus, I dismissed a whole host of honourable gentlemen in my romantic journey, for fear of becoming a trophy wife.

Moreover, I developed a knack for seeking out losers. There was no way I was going to wait for them at the prison gates, but if there was a social case study to fall in love with, I was there. My legs still bare and my head still held high. No doubt I had buried deep within me the need to justify my rathole genes. Or to despise "the bunch of pigs", namely the boys from good families, who were the only ones who could afford my splendour. My flirtations at the time panicked my grandfather who, however, never reprimanded me. Dad waited for me to mature. Mum, on the other hand, demoralised that my designs were outperforming her wishes, made it known to me violently.

Among the chosen ones, my first adolescent

thrills attached themselves to a loudmouth high school student four years my senior. As his friends proved more brilliant than he in delivering socio-political Marxist tirades, he ripped into my stupidity instead, becoming more and more enamoured with each of his ridiculous outbursts. I went with him to Geneva, in search of the Landolt brasserie that Lenin had frequented, but also to numerous demonstrations. Legs still bare, head still held high, and dressed all in red. Languid as could be! Yet I suffered, because when it came to cuddles, he preferred revolutionaries more inclined to take their knickers off in attempts to free themselves from the yoke of abominable capitalism. While I just played the *virgin fatale* in the antechamber of Love with a capital L!

I adored his little brother, a ten-year-old kid with a cherubic face. He had a dog, and together we went for walks in the Juran forests. He would be one of the first to be struck down by AIDS. Living in agony in a hovel of a home with his mother, an off-the-grid Russian woman, always with a book in her hand. Before the two of them died in a fire in that cursed rathole...

I shared a romantic connection with my revolutionary's best friend. He was an artist who designed jewellery for a famous firm. One day, he showed up at our house. Mum was alone at home. He told her he'd come to ask for her daughter's hand in marriage! Mum laughed:

"My dear boy, ask her yourself!"

However, she thought he was cute...

He was cute. But I was in love with the Marxist!

Sometime later, this friend met a young woman who was just about to get married. It was love at first sight and they moved in together. As for the cuckolded fiancé, he surprised him one evening and smashed his jaw in. The two lovers reacted with even more passion! I saw much less of him until a certain tragedy, one November evening. He caused an accident that cost his beloved her life. He never recovered and became dark and morose. Often drunk, high even. For the drugs of the liberation years were beginning to wreak havoc in the working-class city and spared no segment of the population.

One evening, the three of us were there, as usual. Dinner at the Morose One's house, with hashish and LSD for dessert. I'd never taken this kind of substance. I wasn't convinced, but I was intrigued. All the walls were covered with huge black-and-white portraits of the deceased. The setting was almost macabre. With legs bare and my head held in a foggy high, I smoked my first joint, which had no other effect than to make me giggle like a fool. That's when the Holy Grail was brought out. Three lozenges that looked like the mints I'd suck to get seductive breath. My two companions swallowed theirs…

I can still see myself, leaning out the window with mine in the palm of my hand. The Morose One encouraged me. I hesitated. Just when I was determined not to back down, my Marxist, who ordinarily wasn't the blueprint of an understanding gallant, murmured:

"If it doesn't feel right, don't take it!"

When I think of the scene that followed, I can only be grateful! The Morose One fell prey to terrible hallucinations. He fell into wild incoherent screams, through which his love's first name was heard as he crashed against the walls! Before collapsing, moaning, onto his bed…

We left him, and in the middle of the night I went back home with my revolutionary, who was convinced he was a large swallow!

I never touched drugs again…

Shortly after, the Marxist left for Paris. The Morose One went to France too. They were lost from view…

During an evening with a group of friends pretending to be rock stars, I met the archetypal short-ass. A kind of weasel who fancied himself as a bit of a pretty boy and who had taken it into his head, or rather, into his balls, to deflower me. Mum's repulsion towards him and the ban on meeting him gave wings to my appetite for the forbidden. I half-gave in. During a miserable night. On a miserable couch. With pitiful performances! Once I had crossed the line, I felt my own worthlessness as much as his and I returned to more stellar loves. With a hobo from the most disadvantaged neighbourhood in the city. Mother abused, of course, by an alcoholic father. When he wasn't wandering the pavements, he was banging a lacklustre beat on a drum kit with a lacklustre band in a lacklustre bar. It was there, one Saturday evening, that I chose to show off my bare legs and my freshly touched-up platinum hair dye. Enough to hold my head high, always and forever. His face had a soothing finesse. His eyes were engulfed by a touching melancholy. Like any artist worthy of the name, he had long hair. Reddish brown. Without hesitation, with my legs very bare and my head very high, I offered him a cajoling friendship. I planned to convert him to studying to be a jeweller. Since he was already making silver jewellery. Too heavy for my fingers and wrists, that nevertheless had new pieces added to them every week. Sometimes, I invited him to come take a bath in the family bathtub. He never took advantage of this arrangement and came out of the bathroom each time in his floral shirt and jeans.

We kissed. Often. I loved kissing him. When winter came, he held me close in his camel hair coat. He idolised me. I felt a mixture of compassion and tenderness. An infatuation bordering on pride for my social work and my snub to the bourgeoisie that, like any 1968er, I had vowed to mock. One day, without ever having set foot in art school or a jewellery store, he decided to leave for Morocco. Just to give us time to take stock. I detached the coral Buddha medallion from around my neck to attach it to his. The final vibration of the farewell kiss...

Crimes, drugs, arrest. Instead of taking stock, he found himself clenching his fist in a so-called correction facility. For months, I received admirable love letters. Small objects too that he made in his workshop, including a varnished wooden frame onto which he had glued a four-leaf clover. One day I met him again, just after I had hooked up with the most famous athlete in Switzerland, ten years my senior:

"At least he's a man," he sighed, his eyes more melancholy than ever. A few years later, I learned he hadn't survived a heroin overdose. A dramatic romance that forever left me with a sense of wanting to fight against the inequality at our starting lines.

As unthinkable as it might have seemed to any groupie of the time, I hesitated for several weeks before having a coffee with the legendary stadium star. Until that day when... I found him looking crestfallen. My consent stemmed from both the promise of a possible new rescue, but also a flattered curiosity about the man whose name I chanted as a child with thousands of fans at matches. I discovered the reason for his lifeless appearance shortly after, namely a suicide attempt in the middle of a divorce that had deprived him of his three-year-old daughter. Thus began my Odyssey with this hero who was making the headlines. As if destiny was whispering that I should repair a hurt, just as it was absenting itself from the nursing home where Bluette had once stayed...

18
My First Marriage

With my legs still bare, and my head still held high, I began studying literature at the University of Neuchâtel. In my free time, I answered phones for a watchmaking firm. The big boss there sent me, very bare-legged, to the Basel fair, where I did not fail to impress some clients. More with my super-tight knitted purple dress than with my business knowledge. Then upon my return, the same boss suggested I could "launch myself into international trade" by modelling my career on his experience. But I wasn't ready to abandon Balzac, Hugo, and Baudelaire. Without having a shadow of an ounce of it, I was preparing to cross the threshold of maturity. Confident in my lucky stars and in this world that was, at least a little, finally at my feet. I was going to leave the quartet to create my own.

The first flames of our love were, as is often the case, pleasant. Restaurant meals, a trip to London for my 20th birthday, fashion boutiques so that my starlet features would measure up more closely to those of a star's girlfriend. When he was playing matches away, I had the keys to the Mini Cooper and then the Lancia coupé. I strutted around, nothing more. Unconscious, nothing less. His virility, as a fully signed-up male, shook me rather than delighted me. To the point of making me miss my soft toy rabbit:

"Is that all there is to it?" I sometimes wondered.

Little by little, I discovered more about what he had described in an interview as being a "fourth-class Swiss". He had escaped from the same rat-holes that had made the little Suzanne shudder…

His mother, a great mass of self-denial, was as resigned as she was resilient. Brave, hardworking, with a huge smile that she wore like a valiant sword against filth and poverty. I loved her, and I regret not having found the moment to tell her so…

His father dismantled engines and resold the scrap metal. A hard worker who loved his alcohol, that fleeting freedom of the poor...

Drunk, one morning he slaughtered his son's puppy to eat it. The image of this little boy who often looked after pigs during school hours, disfigured by the ordeal of finding his only companion on the Sunday table, shook my heart. And I resolved to stay, for better or for worse. Admiring his fury to get by, to the point of his running through the woods with kilos of weight. In pursuit of a career that would elevate him to the top, regardless of his academic shortcomings. Unfaithful, he told me about his lovemaking with a prostitute in Japan during his participation in the Olympic Games. I swallowed the bitter pills as he experienced multiple breakups. He always came back for me, but I was floundering far from the Pierre-André and Suzanne duo. However, I didn't cheat on him. Only just though! Holidaying on our island paradise, while he was in England, I flirted with a German student whose sensitivity was attractive to me. So much so that I had felt ready to attract him in turn, on the very day my hero surprised me by turning up. With the proposition of moving to German-speaking

Switzerland, because he had just changed clubs...

At the end of this ruined holiday, I moved, half-convinced, and enrolled at the University of Zurich. Today, I am stunned by my inability to resist life's obstacles. Even so, my instinct for independence did urge me to look for a job alongside my studies. Private French lessons at a renowned institute. Insecure, the hero rushed into asking me to marry him. My little bird brain convinced itself it knew what it was doing. Or rather, it didn't have the crib sheet to ask itself questions about what it really wanted. So, legs bare and head held high, I got married. Civilly, at the Zug town hall. Secretly, almost, so that journalists wouldn't bother us. A flash of foreboding was sparked as I made out the French words on my students' congratulatory bouquet:

"We wish you lots of luck in your life together!"

It was all written:

Our life was never "together"!

One day, he took his daughter on vacation. An adorable eight-year-old. Perfectly behaved. Funny. Sweet. At the end of the trip, he plotted to avoid sending her back to her mother on the other side of France. The girl then asked me:

"If I stay, do you want me to call you Mum?"

I was deeply moved, yet unsettled. I was part of a saga that seemed to be unfolding without my knowledge.

At least I had successfully completed my teaching diploma and was working hard at the high school. Situated on a small hill that quickly became my hill. A few kilometres from the battle of the 1,500 Confederates who, in 1315 at Morgarten, had gallantly put to rout more than 4,000 Austrians. It was the first time my Swiss nationality resonated within me, and I felt the armed struggle for freedom, democracy, and a nation's survival inhabiting me. As I taught my students, I was inhabited by John Nussbaum, Yves Velan, and Edgard Tripet too. The rest was marital infrastructure of little importance...

One evening, I was reading a story to my future adopted daughter. The doorbell rang. She rushed to the door, and I heard her shout, "Mum!" That cry suggested to me that this was something serious, and I took on a level of maturity.

Violence between the two parents, which my

new maturity badge gave me authority to reprimand as I stood facing the overwhelming spectacle. I wept for a long time when the judge ruled that the little girl would go back to her mother: "Don't cry, we'll have more children..."

Back problems, a desire to dissect the geography map, and a jealousy over the enthusiasm my students showed me, led him to give up sport. He bought an old VW campervan. Once he had converted it, we would join hippies on the road. A globetrotter in my blood, I finally felt invested in my relationship. I hoped for the best. However, after closing my bank account, I took care to sew 1,500 Deutsche Marks into the lining of my jacket. The Deutsche Mark being a safe and stable currency, I could use it to desert the campervan just in case...

In tears, I left my students. A heartbreak far crueller than I had imagined...

We set off as far as Afghanistan. Later, we hit North Africa. Seeing our campervan, with its mini-fridge, its curtains, or its small sink, the indigenous people shuddered. As for me, I managed without a shower or a toilet. Save for a hazy episode at the Turkey-Iran border. An endless line of trucks was waiting there. With us in the middle. I made my way down the line to ask one of the drivers if there were toilets. Laughing, he and his companions pointed out a shed, and I found myself in a vast room where everyone had deposited their excrement on the floor. I did the same, before going back out with my head held high despite the sniggers.

We took turns driving. Our conversations revolved around the organisation of the trip. Sometimes about the people we met or the risks we faced. We ate meals consisting of various soups, of which we had brought kilos in powder form, condensed milk, pasta, and potatoes. Plus a few local products from the markets because our budget had to last a long time. Around our bed, there was a bookshelf with the books I had brought. Mainly Baudelaire, *The Little Prince*, and Camus. I'd also started a journal. The landscape that captivated me was in Turkey, at the edge of the still-barren steppes. Mount Ararat, where Noah's Ark seemed to have run aground. Reunions with my mystical old flames. I moved forward, gripped by a feverish fascination, both hands on the steering wheel of our four-wheeled lodging. Before me, the divine summit of the world, from where humanity had been given the chance to start again from scratch!

To start from scratch...

My second communion with the mystical impulses of my adolescence took place in Istanbul. The Blue Mosque, near which we were parked with other escapees bound for Asia, reframed me in a carillon of energy. As for the Hagia Sophia, it rekindled my attraction to the sacred. A density of prayers that had managed to survive massacres. Forever engraved in these walls, surrendered to successive conquerors of the city that one day I would only call Constantinople. My eternal Constantinople...

Iran. In that October of 1975, I wandered around in Tehran as though it were Zurich, chatting with brilliant students as liberated as they were ravishing...

My third spiritual inspiration sprang from the other end of our road map, in the middle of the Moroccan desert. The Tuaregs of Morocco made my mystical nostalgia resurface. Our dishevelled men in ripped jeans and faded T-shirts appeared to me like clumsy buffoons next to these princes on their dromedaries. I imagined them all to be noble. All wise men. Conversing in their silent magnificence with only the stars and the spirits of the dunes. I wanted to abscond. To leave with them. To head towards that line where the sky still whispered to the earth how beautiful it found it. Perhaps because it was a time when it was still beautiful, even if we already sensed that these virgin horizons would soon be violated. By luxurious hotels of tumultuous ugliness. Morocco, with its credulous smiles, carried me away to a land of fairies. I was bewitched by the captivating gazes. What had become of all those mysterious eyes? In a world that moves too fast and only knows how to shout...

However, since the fairies hadn't planned on feeding us, we had to think about the future. After a trip to Switzerland to inquire at the consulate about teaching opportunities, we left for London. My hero, who was fluent in English, took his large tape recorder with him. Above all, he planned to learn to write correctly in one of the three national languages he spoke. French, since that was my specialty. I planned to earn an English proficiency certificate, while giving conversation lessons in a London school. In a desolate and desolated suburb, as it turned out. Not only did I never get paid there, but I was wasting time teaching from my own essays, which the urchins in Her Majesty's Kingdom couldn't care less about. One day, arguments exhausted, I shouted at them:

"What are you talking about?"

"Men..."

Well, they couldn't have said it at a better time! With my legs still bare and my head held less and less high, I gave up on sharing my treasured experiences with them. About to face one of those setbacks we call a point of no return.

One evening, I saw my hero struggling up the stairs. He had just had a vasectomy. Thanks to the generosity of England in the 1970s:

"So you won't need to take the pill anymore!"

"Oh... Great! And... Does it hurt?"

Without waiting for an answer, I left. I can still see myself, ponytail blowing in the wind, hurtling through that London suburb, crying. Without really understanding why, against what, or against whom...

I decided to abandon the capital to devote myself solely to my studies. I just wanted to move on. We left without ever mentioning the vasectomy again, in the chiller you had to put coins in for a little heat. Off to Cambridge. I enrolled in a language school there. I failed the entrance exam for the proficiency classes, but I got the principal to let me skip a grade. I assured him that I would work day and night in our student flat. Promise kept...

What a delight! A friendly class, two competent teachers, one of whom, Paul, was cheerful, disarmingly gentle, and had hair that was always a mess. I fell in love with him and confided this to him in an over-the-top essay. I remember describing him as someone so balanced that my heart felt how adrift it was.

I had crossed my Rubicon...

My legs still bare and my head much lower, I became aware of how suffocated I was. A doctor I consulted for stomach aches diagnosed me with depression. So I treated myself with the only therapy available to me: work. More than ever, I invested myself in my studies. The hero, for his part, was making unexpected progress that, once again, earned my admiration. But he was struggling too...

After the last exam, and completely drunk, I climbed with some classmates into a boat along the Cam. I was belting out songs by Brel and Piaf. My hero greeted me at the end with my passport in his hand:

"Your passport, I'm going home, you sort yourself out!"

I was wearing my jacket with the 1,500 Deutsche Marks. So, my feeling of intoxication only intensified as for the first time I smelled freedom. But he changed his mind. So it was Together that we set off once more on the road home.

And this time, the worst lay ahead of me...

19
Divorce

He still held currency as a celebrity and this opened doors to a boarding school reserved for wealthy foreigners in a splendid resort in French-speaking Switzerland. He was assigned to sports and to working within the senior management team. His reputation, his candid attitude, his experience, his mastery of four languages, and his undeniable charisma contributed to this meteoric rise. Still, I hadn't followed him to do nothing! For my part, I taught French and German in English. Our salaries were average, but there were no expenses. We were fed at the boarding school and housed in a sumptuous chalet facing the Alps. The evening we moved in, I was already swimming in the huge pool, surrounded by nature. It was enough to make me feel like I was in the gardens of paradise, even without a soft toy bunny…

There were summer courses before the start of term, and I returned to that profession that I was so passionate about. Our life was communal until the evening meal. Which saved us from being left alone with each other with so little or nothing left to share. Except for the muffled despair of shared loneliness. That insidious constraint that means that when you utter a word, even a banal one, it's another that's heard. So I swallowed, I swallowed down my words, my feelings, my desires, my tears. I swallowed myself. I swallowed myself whole…

One evening, the principal passed me in the garden. More swallowed down than ever:

"You're welcome here, at our place, it's international. Something a bit different from your little family institute in German-Switzerland!"

I don't remember what I said. I think I smiled, as he had just managed to pierce open the wound that needed to be compressed, squashed down, cauterised. I couldn't care less about internationalism; a family was exactly what I wanted. The one I didn't have. And above all, I needed to rediscover my passion. The legacy of

John Nussbaum, Yves Velan, and Edgar Tripet. And his words were the catalyst I needed!

So it was that, at dawn the following Sunday, I slipped into my brand-new Mini and ventured over the mountain passes to get to my hill. My little hill that I had left in tears two years earlier. I was wearing my light-coloured suit and new shoes. My legs were still bare, but my head was in pieces.

I knew the routine. The principal, whom we called the *"boss"*, was on duty on Sundays. It was striking noon as I climbed the stairs leading to his private apartment. I arrived at the door just as he was leaving to go to lunch with the students. Never… never have I encountered such a look, telling me that he had simply understood. While he hadn't approved of my hippie exodus, he had managed to discern what no one else knew. This young woman in her elegant suit, with her gleaming shoes, her bare legs, her blonde hair, was a woman drowning.

He murmured:

"You've lost weight…"

Together, we crossed the corridor that they called "Klostergang" towards the dining hall. I inhaled my scents. My bearings. Then we spent the afternoon in his office. Where once I had come to complain, ask for advice, announce my exodus. I didn't notice the hours passing as one by one he cracked open the locks on my heart. I told and told and told. In no particular order, I unpacked what I had been swallowing down, repressing for too many years. It was the first time in my life that I realised how urgent, how essential, how vital it is to speak out:

To speak out and be listened to.

He got it!

He would let me come back, on the condition that this time I would stay. He also offered my hero refresher courses working with the PE teacher. Towards evening, he walked me back to the front steps. He took both my hands in his:

"We're going to make a great life up here!"

I wished this goodbye could last forever...

Exhausted but wrapped up in a delicious tranquility, I drove legs bare and head up towards the great resort. Determined to make my choice. But instead of meditating on "the great life," that night I was to discover just why the word "duty" had been added to the word "marital"...

The next day, I called the boss to say that we would both be arriving for the start of the school year in September. That's when we abandoned international travel for the Alps...

Summer passed. Time to find accommodation by the lake. And for me, to feverishly study books on pedagogy, in order to be up to the task. Filling a thick binder with a literature course, so as to immerse my students in the soul of the language of Voltaire that I was getting ready to teach them...

At the beginning of September, my legs still bare and my head still held high, I went into my classes, my heart exploding with projects. Following in the footsteps of John Nussbaum, Yves Velan, Edgar Tripet... And my disarming Cambridge Paul!

The still-notorious hero abandoned his refresher classes in favour of private sports lessons in town. Meanwhile, my integration, body and soul, into the family business was instantaneous. Of course, not everything was perfect, not by a long shot. I made many rookie errors, but I felt at home. More than ever, or for the first time, at home. My existence could be summed up in one word: work.

As for my so-called emotional life, it slipped from my horizon. It should be noted that being a boarding school teacher, a class teacher, and subject to yearly state exams with a minimum pass level, was not a long, quiet river. I worked intensely and needed all my energy. If I didn't have a Caesar Hannibal, I became the confidante of many students. Including young girls, who were increasingly numerous in this all-boys boarding school.

Inevitably, this 300% absorption threatened to lead us into our first battles. Jealousy is its name. To the reproaches were added the interrogations. He checked the mileage on my car's odometer to work out whether or not I was meeting a potential lover. The accusations piled up, more and more pressing. Oppressing. It's undeniable that the stadium hero was suffering. That I felt a thousand miles away from his suffering. That I had always felt a million miles away from his clandestine distress. And of course, a million miles away from the marital bliss of my dreams. We no longer had anything in common since we sold the VW campervan. And nothing could replenish this dried-up abyss...

One evening, I had a meeting with a difficult class. Two of my colleagues were assisting me. I had taken one of them in my Mini to a mountain chalet. I remember there was a terrible thunderstorm on the way back. I was bending over backwards not to crush the frogs and zigzagging through the lightning while my teammate yelled. Then we chatted, untying the evening's knots. Little by little, confidences about our private lives emerged. His seemed mediocre. Mine bordered on the labyrinthine...

When I got home, very late, he was waiting for me. On the living room table, I saw the big tape recorder from Cambridge. Without saying a word, I ran a bath to warm myself up. He followed me saying:

"I have said it all, explained it all, and it's all recorded..."

I'll never know how I ended up dripping and naked, screaming in the corridor, while he struggled to drag me back into the apartment. A titanic force, pushing me under the water of that bathtub that should have been my tomb. The landlady's Great Dane, who lived on the floor below, was the first on the scene. I knew him well. I often took him for walks in the fields. I learned later that he hadn't slept that evening, unusually agitated. His owner took me in. I collapsed. Submerged. Just not drowned. Submerged by madness. By male strength. By brutality.

But also... By life. By my life! I spent the rest of the night with my vigilant saviour. In the morning, I called the *boss* to ask him what I should do:

"Come back to take your classes, it will be your victory!"

The old lady ventured upstairs and brought me some clothes. My tormentor seemed devastated, overcome with regret...

My blonde tresses out of the water, I found myself in front of my classes. With a Moroccan silk scarf around my neck. No one noticed a thing. After class, I collapsed for a long therapy session in the famous office. It was then the boss's turn to make me forget the shadow of death...

He told me an intimate anecdote that bordered on both the burlesque and the sublime:

"A few days ago, I travelled 150km to visit my brother and his wife. He's an alcoholic. The apartment was cluttered with empty bottles. Piled up. They were everywhere. So I put them in plastic bags in the boot of my car. And I hit the road again. It was getting dark. It started to snow. It was snowing heavily. I wondered what I would do with my load. Then every time I saw a litter bin I stopped to throw one of those bags in. I was desperate, I said to myself, 'Thank goodness no one can see you!' A storm whipped up. I was scared and I prayed. I begged God to send his angels to guide me..." There was a long silence. He had a knack for orchestrating silences. For making them full: "It was after that, with Saint Michael the Archangel on the left side of my car and the Archangel Gabriel on the right, that I was able to return safely."

He then stood up and traced a cross on my atheist forehead with his thumb:

"From now on, I will pray that they are with

you!"

Thank you, Dietmar, thank you...

As astonishing as it might seem, I went home. The stadium hero explained to me that he was convinced I had a lover, that he would never do it again...

I didn't have a lover!

But lover or not, the boundary had been crossed, without even yet knowing the scars this attempt had engraved in my soul. After hiding a knife under my radio-alarm clock for nights, I made an appointment with a lawyer. The weeks that followed were hellish. It went without saying that I could no longer imagine the slightest physical connection. That's when I fell upon scandalous newspaper articles scattered everywhere. About desperate men who had murdered their unfaithful partners. Pornographic magazines that also suggested to me that male rights were not a thing of the past. One evening, coming home from class, I was forced to fulfil my marital duty. I think I would have preferred him to stick pins in my head! When I got up to wash, I was bleeding. The next day, exhausted and on the brink of collapse, I took refuge with a friend of the *boss*. Safe and sound, I called the man who was still my husband:

"It's me ... Are you okay?"

"No, because you left me! Tomorrow you'll find me hanged in your classroom!"

The next day, before the students arrived, I went through all the classrooms before calling his sister, who managed to reach him.

He was asleep.

I never saw him again...

He emptied the apartment and fled abroad. A ploy to prevent me from getting a divorce. I got it in his absence...

Today, I sincerely hope he found his share of happiness. It takes two to make a youthful mistake, and it's clear I lacked the maturity to manage someone even more messed up than me. It's called life experience...

The *boss* released me a little before the Easter break. I would go and recover at my parents' house. In the garden facing the Jura. It was there one rainy morning that I learned I had passed my proficiency exam. I knelt in the soaking wet earth.

My legs bare, my head hanging as low as possible, and I began to sob. Sob the deluge out of my body. Until I was wrung dry. It was the smell of the earth that inspired me to start over.

To start from scratch? Do we ever start over, or do we continue with our more or less closed wounds? In my case, there were more open than there were closed.

Forty-five years later, I feel that we don't descend from the ark of our traumas like Noah from Mount Ararat. We move forward, but we still have to want to. With words, listening, and with the desire for reconciliation. Purifying our hearts of the cancer of resentment by accepting that something has been destroyed. I still tremble when a man walks behind me at nightfall. Which doesn't stop me from walking. Accepting doesn't mean clinging to wounds obsessively or... gaining some kind of advantage from them. There are many pitfalls along the path of such endless asceticism...

If I didn't start over from scratch in the garden facing the Jura, I had a job, a considerable capacity for effort, friends, a nice face. A beauty queen's figure, after all, I had won that competition and paraded through the watchmaking town on a flower-covered float! A brand-new proficiency certificate, and above all...

Above all... After the rage to survive, I had the rage to live...

20

Journeys

In a fit of frustration, the stadium hero had cursed me: "I hope one day you'll be very sick!" A curse fulfilled, as I describe in my book, *Illness, My Complicit Enemy.* Hepatitis C, long ignored, resulted in a permanent exhaustion. Aside from obligatory outings with students or colleagues, I was never able to go out to the cinema, the theatre, or a concert. I led a spartan life. Later, breast cancer, two back operations... A pile of ground meat. However, just not enough to let go. *C'est ça*, the rage to live! I'd probably already acquired it at the moment I was conceived, because Mum swallowed a few Kenyan potions during the abortionist's vacation. And already, I wasn't giving up...

Before my divorce was finalised, I made up for

lost excitement with a student at Zurich University. I gave him private lessons. French, of course! Just fabulous. Reassuring. Enchantingly sweet. We swore we'd love each other so much that the angels would be jealous. I adored his mother. She was sensitive and full of humour. With an expression full of emotion when faced with our love. We had already chosen the name of our future little boy. In short, the whole kaboodle. Except that his father, a wealthy businessman, notable and noted, was hatching a very specific plan for our relationship. So I ended up letting him simmer over his son's future without me. Regaining my beloved autonomy, even though I struggled during this breakup. Another opportunity to bring out my rage to live…

There followed a series of torpedoed encounters but the sparks didn't turn into flames. Faced with the incompatibility of joining epicurean Taurus with tormented Scorpio rising. Tormented by an obsession with the fusion between the burning desert and the mystical skies of its nights. These nips in the bud, so to speak, are summed up in this sentence from a suitor. A fiery Apollo, married and tired of his sweetheart's services. Desperately in love, he offered me the keys to a villa and a luxury car to:

"Wake up with my amber hair on his chest!"

Which is quite an expensive way to wake up in anyone's language!

Faced with my refusal, without me even having deigned to assess the value of the goods, and therefore my own, he concluded:

"You have been touched by grace!"

Above all, I clung to my independence. It's obvious that my profession and the high salary it rewarded made my job easier.

Other, less sales-oriented, people proposed marriage to me. The widowed or divorced fathers of my students, often too well-off for my genes. They were politely dismissed. I then focused on platonic love:

Paris by night for purified lovers! Even if it was more out of a fear that the conflagration of the bodies wouldn't match up to the elevation of the soul. Of course, like any fucked-up thirty-something, I also rejected many suitors for what is called an "ick"...

At work, I became the queen who was heckled but adored by my mostly male colleagues, whose manner of speaking I adopted. Some became close friends, including our old biology teacher. His love life was as chaotic as mine. We shared a common pursuit of beauty, a passion for nature and wildlife, which he explained to me during trips to the forest. Over the years, we would sometimes spend the night after a party in one another's cars, regardless of the outside temperature, in conversations that had a rare authenticity. My old Toni, I will never forget you...

Crammed into a cramped staff room, we formed a community, roped together. Sometimes on days when the foehn wind was blowing, the lid of the pan would explode. We would argue. But we also shared so much laughter, worries, dramas, and complicity. Craziness. Boarding school life, relationships of an intensity I never experienced again...

During school holidays, I didn't hold back from travelling:

My first destination was Mombasa. Beaches with stars reflected in the waves. Perhaps they still knew? A few of my colleagues shared a complacent snigger, implying that they knew all about my desire for muscular black cocks. So often we fixate on the bodily because it's the easiest to understand. They were right; I met my first sex tourists there. Or simply those with their own kind of rage to live! For my part, all I wanted was to dive into that warm sea, into the nights of light. To feel them, to smell them. To thank them for having attracted both my parents and my potential abortionist.

In fact, I was somewhat forced to spend my stay in the company of a Ticino mechanic and his daughter. We were the only ones who didn't have our visas as we disembarked from that giant DC-10. The police officer, after the bus had taken the other passengers to the hotel, questioned me assiduously before releasing it to me. He insisted on showing me around Kenya. At that point I pretended I was there with a friend and his daughter. They played along. That evening, in my room, the phone rang. A muscular cock wanted to have a drink by the pool. So at breakfast, I sat at the father and daughter's table and I stayed there until the end of the vacation. It was with them, too, that I toured the country. In any case, I didn't need solitude to experience the splendour my parents had described, nor the joie de vivre of their Shangri-La.

For my next holiday, I flew to Sri Lanka in search of Buddhist monks. After finding myself face to face with a fat, laughing monk in a lotus position on a stool, the only piece of furniture in a room I'd wandered into without permission, I abandoned the monks. And I fell in love with elephants. But I do have one memory of an idyllic spiritual evening:

Three temples side by side: Buddhist, Hindu, and Catholic. Three paths. Outside each of them, followers of the three religions advancing with their offerings in serene devotion…

In the summer, I went camping alone in Corsica. Not exactly relaxing, as I felt neither safe from the crawling insects nor from the night when the brush crackled…

Later, I left Varna, Bulgaria, for 1980's Russia. My head still high and my legs still bare. Since I no longer had the bleached mop of hair, I had great difficulty getting through customs with my passport photo. Another passenger in the group was turned away. The soldier, who was outraged by this change to my appearance, stood up. He was wearing very high boots. He asked me to walk backwards and forwards in front of him. And I had the nerve to say in French, which fortunately he didn't speak: "Honestly, doesn't playing the clown like that remind you of something?" Head high, legs bare. Light-hearted. There must be a fairy watching over the unselfconscious!

Arriving at a Moscow hotel building, I was surprised to be given a double room, with the only other single person in the group, an Egyptian man. The hotel employee didn't bother listening to my complaint, so I sat on the steps, proclaiming I would spend the night there. It was our tour guide who welcomed me into her room. I proved ungrateful the next day at the Kremlin. After visiting all the glories of the revolution, the churches seemed to have been forgotten. So, when it was time to continue the tour, which was meant to keep to schedule and stay in one group, I announced with my head high and legs bare:

"I have my passport, I'm trilingual, continue the

itinerary without me, I want to find out about the culture of the Holy Russia too!"

Luckily, a German woman exclaimed:

"Bravo, Little Swiss, I'm with her!"

And finally, the whole group came with me to admire the cathedrals, leaving the dismayed guide waiting for us. Shortly after, I apologised. She simply replied:

"Holy Russia... My starving grandmother was illiterate in it. I have been able to study for free, I have a trade and a job!"

Not another word. That night, when I found myself isolated on the Moscow-St. Petersburg night train, and five drunk yobs took the five remaining berths, I didn't have the courage to go and beg her for help. Fortunately, an English couple took pity on me. The gentleman went to sleep with the vodka drinkers and gave me his bed with his wife.

In the evening, I ventured out alone for an after-dinner walk. With the feeling that I was always under someone's gaze...

Yet I loved the frescoes and icons of that Holy Russia. The few I managed to visit. I was moved on the return flight when, before boarding an ancient propeller plane, the old communist matushkas crossed themselves in the gangway. How distant and unreal it seems to me today. What happened to my guide? Has her son gone to war? Or is he one of those super-rich businessmen arrogantly flaunting their fortunes in Limassol or elsewhere? Perhaps he has become a priest in the Church of Holy Russia? One of those village priests removed from political shenanigans, who loves his flock and takes care of them with devotion...

21

My Little Hill

No matter the trip, it was always with emotion that I'd return to my little hill. The sessions in the boss's office soothed me when my balance was shaky. The *boss* who taught me my craft. The art of convincing a teenager who was insecure:

"You can do it, you will!"

Managing relationships with parents and colleagues. Agreeing to work together with those whose points of view opposed mine. According to his motto:

"No unity of doctrine, but all united behind one another!"

Thus, he authorised a Jewish colleague to not wash or shave for a week after his father's death:

"This way, the students will have the widest possible range of diverse personalities!"

What a visionary, obsessed with the power of unity. Unity in diversity. How many practise such a thing in business or politics? This crucifixion brought its own fruits. He didn't hesitate in appointing a brilliant bulldozer as his deputy head, a man who made no secret of his political leanings, which were opposed to his own. The *boss* also had this ability to roll with the punches, managing the overwhelming enthusiasms of each protagonist. What a tireless commitment to understanding our weaknesses. And to covering them up. He didn't always hide his own, by the way. Especially during those drunken evenings. His outbursts of anger are as memorable as his outbursts of generosity. He knew how to correct my exuberant outbursts, relics of May 1968. Above all, he instilled in me a love of work and the determination to never give up on a problem. Over time, he became part of my *destiny*, like one of those trusty pillars. My best ally. The best ally I've ever had in my life. So when illness took hold of his body, it was an earthquake. He announced it to me, calling me in the dead of an icy night.

"It's me..."

His voice was hollow. Then a silence, one of those that portends misfortune:

"I'm very sick..."

I put my heavy coat on over my pyjamas and rushed into my icy car. In the dead of an icy night, on the icy road, towards my icy little hill...

He was waiting for me in the reception room where we used to receive parents. In his dressing gown, a glass of wine in hand, a lit cigarette, which was rare. The prelude, long before it became fashionable among teenagers, to a sleepover. Facing my icy little lake and the icy Alps still black with sleep:

"This idiot in Zurich who performed an ultrasound discovered nodules on my liver!"

The axe had fallen. So, that night, facing the icy Alps, still black with sleep, it was my turn to make him forget the shadow of death...

It was only later, in the middle of summer, that the unpronounceable word was spoken. I had gone to meet him at the Lukas Clinic in Arlesheim. We were strolling through the Goetheanum. On moving further into that kind of large skull, I felt the moment had come:

"It's cancer, isn't it?"

"Yes..."

I can't say what we visited. We wandered around the building. He sometimes joked or expressed a wish:

"You belong at the foot of my deathbed..."

When he returned home, to my little hill, I accompanied him on a pilgrimage to Einsiedeln to see the Black Madonna. I went back there alone, later, during his dying days. He was in his room just above the classrooms, on his deathbed. That bed he had wished me to be at the foot of...

Thanks to his son, who had left a note in the staff room warning staff not to go to the apartment, I was allowed in. One evening as I was leaving, justifying myself as respecting his father's wishes, he said to me:

"You're not one of the teachers..."

Thank you, Gerhard!

Until his last hours, I was able to hold his hand...

Shortly before he fell into a form of coma, he murmured:

"What a life, what a destiny!"

I knew snippets of his life. A mother who was of the people, simple and gentle. A scholarly father. A very stubborn person who, whatever the weather, would walk the three-hour journey from Oberägeri to Zug to sit in the cantonal parliament. When Dietmar graduated from high school, he took him to Rome, but on the condition that they visit everything on foot! And then ... the inheritance ... The eldest son hadn't lived up to his hopes. So it was the youngest, the future boss, who was made to take over the business in 1952. He was barely 24 years old. Married to a beloved wife who bore him a daughter and three sons. He tirelessly supported her through her struggles with leukaemia. All the while managing the students, the teachers, his own children, and his pain. Then, at 64, he was diagnosed with liver cancer. He will retain a unique place in my heart for as long as I breathe, and even beyond...

Gerhard, despite his arrogance, reminded me of that kid in shorts, with sadly polite eyes, whom I had passed on the stairs, on my first day at the high school. Then he became my colleague. A philosophy professor, as eminent as a political tribune is today, he strove to educate responsible adults. Free to hold their own opinions, as long as they were debated with conviction. When there was the annual match between the teachers and the high school seniors, he played a fierce, solitary role as goalkeeper. Shortly before his father's slow decline, he had taken up the torch...

"Gerhard is much smarter than me and has read much more than me!" the *boss* had confided to me, when the teenager preparing for his French baccalaureate had devoured Proust with a tenacity that was already non-negotiable. Yet their collaboration, under the jealous gazes directed by others at this crown prince with his self-righteous arrogance, was sometimes complicated. The *boss* was still the patriarch! Few, then, would use their envious frustration to encourage two wounded people to confess the admiration and love they felt for each other...

Orphaned by his mother at 8, by his father at 32, Gerhard almost lost his own life in the 2001 massacre at the Zug cantonal parliament. He was 39. Another strange twist of *fate*, and a remarkable resilience...

While it was on my little hill that I learned to love my Switzerland, it is not quite as unscathed as idyllic postcards suggest…

22
My Father's Baptism

My life as a liberated woman during the Eighties was enviable. Yet my legs still bare and my head still held high yearned for more…

The death of my beloved grandfather André was a wake-up call that I needed, if not to dig through the knots of the past, at least to shake up my comfortable routine. In other words, to look for new troubles! On the first page of the Bible bequeathed by André the Intransigent, I discovered a remarkable prayer of acceptance:

"No prayer, not even the smallest, no tear, not even the most pagan, has ever risen to God without Him rushing to welcome it." Thus had André the Inflexible also experienced the sublime value of tolerance. It was, in a way, my first viaticum…

I sweated over the writings of Annick de Souzenelle, discovered by *chance* in my father's library. There, I felt, for the first time, this calling towards the inner voice. Annick was a close friend of my parents. We met by *chance*. My mother had been putting off going to her conference one Siberian winter evening. Finally, she took her car and ventured out. Annick's words deeply affected her. Shortly after, *chance* took my father to Paris, even though his work usually meant travelling either to the USA or the East. A rendezvous over a meal at a restaurant was arranged: "Two soulmates found each other", Annick would later confess. She often came to stay with us on vacation with her phenomenal husband, Geoffroy. An encyclopedia on heron's legs. He created our astrological charts, among other things. Since the question of *destiny* was nagging at me, I played along. And I must say, he revealed some moving elements to each of us. He was a kind of bridge between heaven and earth. Outside of time. Close to Another, perhaps? Something that would bring my soul peace. Or, even more, feel like the right fit…

One day, we were all sitting in the garden overlooking the Jura Mountains, and my father asked Annick the question that had been bothering me ever since my exchanges with the Count of Todtmoos:

"Annick, what must I do to effect this 'reversal of energies' you talk so much about?"

She always had a manly, confident, and reassuring smile:

"Pierre, you must be baptised!"

Thus, 35 years after having spurned his parents' baptismal pool, my father was baptised in the Orthodox parish of Saint Maire in Lausanne. Annick was his godmother and Geoffroy his godfather. And Mother, baptised as a child thanks to Bertha, settled for an Orthodox confirmation…

23
Bible Basher

Sceptical and wary, I was *destined* to venture into Saint Irenaeus Cathedral one autumn day in Paris. Mainly out of curiosity. The church had been founded by Russian émigrés in 1917, eager not only to share its spiritual treasures with France, but also to encourage the Gauls to reconnect with their Christian roots. I was instantly dazzled by the liturgy…

I plunged soul, heart, and body into the cauldron, and I, who had so reviled bigots, was transformed into nothing less than a Bible basher. The simple reason: I never heard them talk of morality. But of the energies of the Holy Spirit. Of transfigured man. Of transfiguring rites. Of this God who plunges into a man's wounds to raise him up. So that he may stand before Him and creation, of which he must once again become the protective prince. As for the services and liturgies, they cast me back to a magical fairyland.

So I became a Parisian whenever I had the free time. And I literally ran with it. Deciding that there would be no more Caesar Hannibal but that my son would bear the name of the founding bishop of this resurrection of Gallic Christian origins, Eugraph. His successor, of pure tricolour stock, became a friend. He would remain so until his death despite the more oriental turn of my ecclesial epics. Monsignor Germain de Saint Denis, as much praised as rejected, not only extricated me from the conscious and unconscious abjection of the clerical world, but he had this rare gift of bowing before the uniqueness of the Person. Trusting God to free him. His classes, his homilies, his humour, and his much-coveted charm taught me, impressed me, and forever influenced me. Thank you, Monsignor...

In the early 1980s, my friend Sonia and I planned a pilgrimage to Israel. Between our journey in the footsteps of Christ and our week spent at the Red Sea, I fitted in a solo return trip to Paris back to the Cathedral of Saint Irenaeus. To celebrate my first Orthodox Easter. To get a discounted ticket, I asked Monsignor Germain for a student card, since I had just begun long distance theology studies at the Saint Denys Institute. I just needed to make myself a few years younger.

The journey to Jerusalem was fraught with emotion. At the Wailing Wall, where I imagined the Chosen People were also praying for the whole world. At the Tomb of the Crucified, when we collapsed in tears. At the Church of the Visitation with a garrulous Palestinian taxi driver. Fascinated by Sonia's breasts, he didn't hesitate to drive down the steps in his Mercedes. And then that nighttime stroll the two scatterbrains took through the Old City, surprised at not encountering any other tourists. When a group of mourners began to wail, Sonia jumped and sprained her ankle. Then, limping, leaning on me, we crossed the entire city returning to the hotel. On Holy Wednesday, at 3:00 a.m., I ordered a taxi and left for Tel Aviv to catch the plane. It was pitch black. My driver, an old Arab, spoke neither English, nor French, nor German. He indicated at the first turning. I thought: "He's going to stop in the countryside and rape me!"

As it turned out, he indicated at every turning, in the night as dark as it was empty...

There had been attacks, and the security checks were draconian. Poor Sonia – who was taking my main suitcase to Eilat, getting confused that it wasn't hers and that the owner, on an Easter expedition to Paris, would soon be back to pick it up – had to retrieve my scattered belongings after they had been chucked in the air by the security services. As for me, I was stopped and told to explain myself due to my famous student card:

"Are you really under 26?"

A little humiliated that this had been noticed, I played it straight and told the police officer my plan. I was able to board...

When I returned, I treated Sonia to a 40th-birthday car trip through the desert, in search of the red sandstone columns, called Solomon's Pillars. Surprised once more not to encounter any tourists. Perhaps because of Israel's recent annexation of the Golan Heights? In any case, I was excited about my expedition. So excited that I forgot to push the choke button back in on the car dashboard, the one pulled out like a sort of cigar to start the vehicle. Arriving in the middle of nowhere, under a scorching sun, the car started to splutter, then stopped. A good hour later the column we saw wasn't Solomon's but that of jeeps and military trucks.

Before rescuing us, they asked us for the identity papers we'd left in the hotel safe, with my driver's licence. It seemed that we looked as innocent as we did stupid, because they fixed our car, and we were able to go home. Thanks, boys! How has life gone on to treat you? Did you have family martyred on that diabolical October 7th? Are your children, also, wrapped up in heavy uniforms? Are they bombing other children just as innocent as themselves so as not to relive a kind of holocaust? Children of the same father, the epic Abraham, will you one day experience my Sri Lankan bliss: different paths, to different temples, with different offerings under the gaze of the one who fathered Isaac and Ishmael? From the same magnanimous Heavens before this panoply of closely related differences?

24
My Second Marriage

It was while attending his theology class on a subject that fascinated me, namely the energies, that I met my future husband. He had ended up in the church by *chance*, while looking, along with his first wife, for a "French" church in which to baptise their youngest daughter. They had found Saint Irenaeus Cathedral in the Yellow Pages. He went there one Sunday morning. Bishop Jean (Eugraph Kovalevsky) was delivering his homily. He never left his side again. He even became the last priest that Monsignor Jean ordained before his death. I could later see, when Pierre took up the priesthood, that Bishop Jean had passed on to him his charismatic manner of throwing open the church doors. Tearing them down even! Whatever one's vices, appearance, or social status. Defying, if necessary, Christian-Mandarin morality. This is the attitude that will forever remain for me the hallmark of his life as a pastor. Bravo, Love! Bravo! And thank you for all those you welcomed with your generous humour!

During his lecture focused on uncreated energies, he placed emphasis on the date August 6, the great Orthodox feast of the Transfiguration of Christ. The moment on Mount Tabor when Christ unveiled the blinding bomb of his divine nature. And the *coincidence* of August 6 being the date when, in Hiroshima, a bomb of energies was used, in the opposite manner, to annihilate. It obsessed me. Still holding my head high, I jumped bare legged into the whole mess, without having made any huge progress within the realms of maturity!

From our first shared glance, our romance had its twists and turns...

A child of the war, with a largely-absent father, Jean Germain, who drove trains at night and slept during the day, before being held prisoner in Germany. A mother, Germaine, whose communist family was buried with the flag, without a priest of course! She was as admirable as she was admirably frustrated. Intelligent, lively, rightly rebellious, a housekeeper for others and for her home. She had actively participated in the 1936 strikes and, in addition to her sons, raised her two younger brothers, who had become orphans. Along with his uncles, Pierre spent his early childhood under the Bordeaux bombings. When the neighbouring goods depot was bombed 50 metres from their home, Germaine decided to send him to live with his paternal grandparents, Louis and Émilie. Louis, who gave ten years to France, including three years of military service, four years of war in 1914-1918, plus three years of occupation in Germany, was a crossings guard in the scrubland of Corrèze. As resistance fighters would come to call at the crossing station, the German soldiers, fortunately from the regular army, had set up a makeshift infirmary for the wounded in their kitchen. They were always polite.

Little Pierre walked for hours to get to school. Alone. Sometimes when the tension was too intense, his grandparents, whom he loved with all his heart, would give him a mess tin and urge him to hide in the forest. Alone. So when he returned to Bordeaux after the war, the boy who would remain, deep down, a lover of solitude, was terrified by the crowded din of the city. In 1945, a little brother, Jacques, was born. I rarely met him, given our hectic and geographically distant lives. I miss him. He was a man with a sharp sense of humor. A caring man.

Thanks to his mother's tenacity, Pierre was able to study engineering in Angers. Then in Paris, at the university campus. At the same time, he tried out for stage roles in various post-war Parisian theatres. Interrupted by enlistment into the Algerian War…

A first union that collapsed without him really realising it. Three teenagers to support…

All we needed to do was match up the wiring of two neurotics…

The wedding photo in the rustic setting of an old priory is filled with light. Even if the teenagers didn't respond to our invitation, which made me once again suspect that a so-called blended family isn't something you arrive at easily.

Yet, I would have so loved to take the youngest with me to study on my hill, while I lived in my chalet. She was 17, and *fate* wouldn't allow it. A divorce is always a difficult ordeal for everyone. They too showed resilience. Despite each other's shortcomings, the geographical dispersion following their father's professional transfer, and the career of their mother, a renowned Gregorian chant artist, Henri, Christel, and Alix all said yes to life!

Our union had to overcome many obstacles, but everything that bound us together forever was inscribed in the most beautiful pages of the book of Heaven. Among the sombre pages, I was definitively deprived of a Caesar Hannibal or a little Eugraph, my breasts not needing in the end to be scratched or mangled. Her children – and probably, in their place, I would have had the same reaction – had other plans. The day he told them about my desire to be a mother, his eldest daughter had cried out: "No, Dad, you're not going to do that again!"

I swallowed it down and swallowed it down...

A few days later, on a pilgrimage to the Virgin

of Cotignac, so that she could bless my womb for a little Eugraph or a little Rebecca, I couldn't bring myself to ask her to "do that again"...

One might wonder if there was a common thread or a correlation between the abortionist's vacation and my inability to become a mother myself?

To close the chapter a few years later, a large fibroid, "my baby", was growing without my knowledge. This time, the "abortionist" wasn't on vacation! The surgeon decided to remove my womb. After the consultation, I ran from the hospital to the parking lot. Just as in London, I ran around crying my eyes out. I was 41 years old...

What remains today of those old lovers Brel sung about?

At times we've sweated through the same pleasures. Worn out the same toilet bowls. At times we've laughed so much. Cried. Waited. We've sometimes argued over ego or selfishness. As we begin the final trajectory, when memories already cross that horizon that no longer returns them, when bodies and souls gather their share of indignities, what remains?

"O Holy Martyrs who suffered valiantly and were crowned, pray to the Lord, that He may save our souls!"

One of the three refrains sung during the Orthodox wedding ritual when the crowned bride circles the Gospel:

Sing together again. With that Tenderness that the years have not managed to erode...

25
The Rage to Live

After the hysterectomy, I was devastated, but more than ever, I still had my dear students! To the point of exhaustion. The weekend trips back and forth to Marseille, where Pierre had been transferred, the gruelling parish commitments, and my full-time job. As my last efforts to cope were being destroyed, I was forced a second time to tear myself away from my beloved high school!

An *unexpected blessing*, as I was harbouring breast cancer...

If departure means dying a little, which was the case, it can also mean the crumbling down of unacknowledged walls. Among them, the revelation of psychotherapy. As soon as we settled in Bordeaux, I began therapy with Professor Gérard Ostermann. Woah, what a defining moment! Again it was *chance* that led me to meet a young woman within the Orthodox parish who was going to his house for her therapy. Convinced not only that the soul nibbles away at the body's energies but that sometimes the body also exhausts the soul's energies, it was he who discovered that I had contracted hepatitis C, the source of many bouts of asthenia. His intelligence, his science and his culture remain for me a lifeline to which I still cling today, when questions arise that others have not even asked. As for the preface that he agreed to write for my book, *Illness, My Complicit Enemy*, not only does it encompass all the content but goes far beyond it.

In the 2000s, I had the huge privilege of mixing analysis sessions, that surgery of the soul, with sacramental confessions that allowed for a certain freedom from responsibility. Father Marc who was assisting in the parish at that time was my confessor. He had the gift of both developing the awareness of where the wrong path was while immersing it in the Love of God. A God who doesn't keep track of sins. In fact, he doesn't care about them, but is happy when we get rid of them, so we can draw closer to Him. Alongside my theology studies in Paris, I returned to my studies in applied psychology. My rage to live never left me. What's more, I cherished it! I was encountering "extraordinary" people in my new world. Among them were Russian émigrés who were still alive. Former nobles who had held onto the nectar of their nobility. I remember four who particularly resonated with my adopted Orthodox soul:

Archbishop Serafim Rodonioff, born in 1905 into a family of Cossack nobles. When I first went to see him, he was still living in Zurich, pastor of the Russian parish of the Resurrection. I asked him to sing Vespers with me in the chapel. He wore his monk's black veil, which I lifted like a bridal train on descending the stairs. It had snowed. The courtyard was white. He stopped:

"My God, Holy Russia..."

I loved listening to him talk about his country. His exile. His arrival by boat in Nice. His art, for he had studied painting. He spoke, alongside Russian, perfect French, English, German, Greek, Italian... One evening, he came at my request to bless the small wooden chalet where I lived. With holy water and a rose in his hand to sprinkle the apartment. I had prepared a fondue bourguignonne for him. But he was disgusted by the raw meat, unable to pierce it with his fork. Funny Cossack! So I roasted him one piece after another. On the other hand, he honoured my bottle of vodka like a true Cossack! He was obsessed with a rapprochement with the Catholics and met Popes Paul VI and John Paul I several times. The most comical memory, which revealed how comfortable he was in his giant frame, occurred in the most chic restaurant in Zurich. My friend Gabrielle and I had invited him to dinner. As he walked through the restaurant, his trousers fell down, and he found himself in his long johns in front of the cream of Zurich society. Armed with that peaceful smile, the one that never left him, he very calmly pulled his trousers back up. A dreamy artist who always knew how to dissect history, both small and large, with wisdom and kindness.

Maxim Kovalevsky, brother of Eugraph, a liturgical composer of unparalleled talent, as enamoured of aesthetics as of tradition. An old friend too, whose kindness revealed the most chivalrous aspects of the human soul. With his immutable delicacy, he amused himself by repeating that "politeness is the best starting point". Or that "preparing a good meal is also part of the Divine plan".

Abbess Olga of the Bussy-en-Othe monastery, who opened her arms and her heart to me, even though she was never embarrassed about shouting me a loud wake-up call. She welcomed me the first time with a group of students for a week of study and sharing, with the blessed collaboration of Hieromonks Josef Pop and Ciprian Span. This Russian émigré was a monument whose gaze, smile, and prayer are unforgettable. One day she confided in me:

"I'm not afraid of death, but of everything that comes before it: illness, hospital..."

On November 3, 2013, at the age of 98, she attended the liturgy for the Feast of the Translation of the Relics of Saint George. After taking communion, she returned to her own cathedral chair and from it went to take communion for eternity...

Finally, the giant theologian, my friend and professor of dogmatics at Saint Sergius, Metropolitan Boris Bobrinskoy. A hurricane of fire and tenderness. Our first meeting was rather stormy. I was waiting by the door at the Saint Sergius Institute for my oral exam in dogmatics. The student before me left after two minutes. Not too reassured, I went in:

"Have you read my book on the Trinity?"

I had studied his lectures but not his book:

"No..."

"Then you can leave, like the student before!"

I went for broke, defying the Slavic colossus:

"I'm teaching all week, I asked for time off for the oral exams, I flew out this morning. I've worked incredibly hard. Test me and send me on my way after that!"

Gauntlet thrown down, the exam began. It started off very badly! I got my head mixed up about the Holy Spirit, so to speak. And for every wrong answer, I was vehemently corrected. Then I got my bearings again. At the end of the interrogation, he said to me:

"You know a lot, you passed, I'm giving you a *quite good!*"

A few weeks later, as I often did, I went to the Bussy-en-Othe Monastery, near where Father Boris had a house. I told Abbess Olga about my exam, my nerves, and my outburst. After the meal, Father Boris, who was holding a service there, approached me:

"I rushed you during the exam. I apologise. Come back and take that oral exam and you'll get a *very good*!

I decided to keep my "quite good" result, but that was the first time that the colossus theologian had moved me with his humility and fatherly affection. It wasn't the last. At each of our meetings, I experienced in action how his immense faith, his equally immense theology, left it to his even more immense heart to give the last word. Thank you, Father Boris, for this inestimable gift!

I was fortunate to have eminent contemporary theologians as teachers among the Gauls too, including another old friend, Father Marc Antoine Costa de Beauregard, whose books I continue to devour.

26
The Jungians

Encouraged by Dr. Ostermann, I also followed a path towards the Jungians, the last of that great Swiss psychiatrist's generation. First, Dr. Roland Cahen, the French translator of Carl Gustav Jung, with whom he became close. In 1936, while undertaking research for his German PhD thesis on Nietzsche's illness, he decided to change direction and study medicine and psychiatry. After attending lectures by Freud, his train stopped in Zurich. There, he met Jung, having only just read his books. He himself went on to comment on this event with these words:

"What do the destinies hold in store?"

After my first analysis session, I felt how much psychoanalysis depends upon a communion of energies between the analyst and the patient, regardless of transference or countertransference. Ostermann was the soothing power of gentleness. Cahen was the volcano. So it was that, in my analysis with him, I had the most violent dream of my life. The last time I saw him, I told him that my husband was an Orthodox priest. Before I left, he grabbed me, shouting: "I'm a priest too!"

Those were the last words I heard him say. I had gone to Paris in early 1998 for my next session with him. The day before the appointment, I received a call that he had left for his final Rendez-Vous...

Finally, there was the day spent with Hélène Hoerni-Jung, Carl Gustav Jung's youngest daughter, in June 2011, thanks to my friend Gabrielle. Gabrielle, a die-hard Jungian who had undergone analysis with Marie-Louise von Franz, Jung's collaborator, is 15 years my senior. I first met her as the mother of one of my students at a Christmas cocktail party. We continued the cocktail party in my car. A true Christmas present. From a woman who saw her father, an Alsatian, forcibly conscripted into the "malgré eux" army when she was four years old. It was the last time she was to wave to him with her little hand, before his heart was forever mutilated by the monstrous war. He was one of those massacred at the Battle of Stalingrad. She never knew the day or the circumstances. It was only recently that she had his name engraved on the family tomb, after arranging a service for his soul. Gabrielle, the wings behind "our work on the soul", since she still practices at 89. At the time, she was following a course on the symbolism of the icon led by Carl Gustav Jung's daughter...

At 97, Hélène Hoerni-Jung radiated undiminished vivacity. She lived in a charming Zurich cottage overlooking the lake. She had baked us a cherry tart. Cherries that still had the flavours of my childhood. I had brought her an icon of the Holy Trinity from Greece, which she received with emotion and a mischievous laugh:

"My son always tells me that instead of dissecting icons, I should venerate them!"

She was a lady. Frail and gentle. Grateful, even though the honour was mine, for the questions I had prepared in advance. Particularly about the role that demons might play in infesting the soul.

She replied that she didn't believe in demons. But also shared her view of the sacraments, of Holy Communion:

"I would never have wanted to receive Holy Communion, because I would have felt like a cannibal!"

She emanated sincerity and intellectual honesty. She confided to us that she hadn't been allowed to study; only her four brothers had. And that when her father was at home on the sofa, buried in his books, the children could have blown the house up, and he wouldn't have noticed a thing. Jung often wrote home while travelling, but he never asked for news of them.

She taught herself, working on the symbolism of icons:

"With a father like that, it's the only field left for me to study!"

A freethinker, she nevertheless considered Jung's "personal myth" to be Melchizedek. A priest beyond time and space. Yet it was Job she evoked when remembering her father. He had suffered the persecutions of his time because of his work. Regarding theology, her father always told her that his writings weren't for Catholic countries (like France) because they had their own rites, rituals, myths, and mysteries...

What would he say today? He didn't reveal anything to us when Gabrielle and I went to recite the "Our Father" at his grave...

I was impressed by the finesse of this young, old writer, her eagerness to make discoveries again and again. But I also felt, as she accompanied us on our return, a spark of anxiety at the answers we never receive. That the lengthening years were beginning to make her impatient...

Helen Hoerni Jung fell asleep three years later, on July 1, 2014, after celebrating her 100th birthday...

These people whom *providence* placed on my path or on whose path I placed myself, because always there is some form of synergy in these things, were each in their own ways chisels with which to carve out my lost soul. Thirst, in cahoots with my rage to live, then pushed me, before I'd crossed the threshold of the second millennium, to drill down into the foundations of orthodoxy...

27
The Byzantine Gift

A never-ending voyage to the origins. We took Greek courses at university before turning to the Byzantine universe. In Greece, we befriended a titan of contemporary theology, the Metropolitan of Nafpaktos, as well as the monasteries he frequented. From our first visit to the Diocese of Nafpaktos, I was captivated by the clarity of his teachings. The one that struck me most was his image of the energies, yes energies again, that have deserted mankind. Because the heart gets smothered on an altar that's covered in ashes. So we fight, that the Holy Spirit might breathe on these ashes. A life-long task. Sin, whose original meaning is to aim badly, corresponds precisely to this loss of energy, every time the heart deviates from the Divine. Nafpaktos had shared a succession of teachings, engraved forever in the blessed book of Transmission. Not to mention that of Friendship too. The book *Orthodox Psychotherapy*, by Metropolitan Hierotheos, a book that Pierre translated into French with exemplary tenacity, remains for me one of the go-to references on therapeutic healing. It was thanks to his translation that Nafpaktos met with us so welcomingly. *Chance* also played its part in the discovery of that book. One day during an unbearably hot Cypriot heatwave, Pierre had picked it up by *chance* in the Larnaca municipal library, where he had taken refuge because they had air conditioning…

Larnaca… My Larnaca! Yes, it is the island of Aphrodite that has the palme d'or. *Cyprus, I Embrace Your Heart,* the title of the book I dedicated to my Cypriot life, speaks for itself. Forever linked to this courageous, funny, and affectionate people. Rooted in the faith transmitted to them by Saint Paul, Saint Barnabas, and Saint Lazarus. Three intense decades, though the conquest wasn't without sweat. When we arrived there in 1999 with our camping tent and a bare minimum budget – I had quit my job, and Pierre was paying for a new training course for his younger sister in Paris – I was far from imagining that this "big rock" would change my heart forever.

What did this Byzantine Orthodoxy bring me, besides the fact that it is, by definition, the canonical church of the apostolic tradition? It can be summed up in eight words:

It put my head back in its place.

The heart, and God knows mine is gifted for this, becomes clogged with all-consuming thoughts that must be constantly tamed. *Voilà* the true, unique, independence, whatever it's wrapped up as. If my head has found its place somewhat, it is also my entire body that has learned to commune with the mysteries. The incarnate bull that I still am likes to stick its snout into relics. Kiss icons. Receive anointing oil. Sniff the scents of incense or flowers adorning the tombs of saints. To engrave the sacred within the body!

During my stays in monasteries, I spent time with monks. Some became "brothers" whose teachings are precious to me. Including teachings on the body, which the great Russian saint Seraphim of Sarov advised treating as one's "best friend". In the refuge of my soul, in the hollow of Mount Troodos, "my monks" taught me, decades after the princes of the desert, that true silence was that of the deep heart. An ephemeral calm each time I'd crossed those stormy dunes of my passions. "My" monks became my magi. They might not be kings. Yet each of them is on a permanent quest for the greatest of kingships:

Humility.

The one I so admire. The one that, despite my significantly lowered whitened head, I do not possess.

On this burning "big rock," the lost soul also fell in love with a people dripping with a joyful, embodied, and living faith. My rage to live has never ceased, never ceases to recharge its batteries there when the burden becomes too heavy. It was in Cyprus, too, that I adopted the first name Maria. Mireille being, in any case, the Provençale version of Mary. And during Byzantine services, my nervous exaltation finally found, finds, and rediscovers deep forgiveness…

It is this very rage to live, that led me to reconnect with writing. It permits me to move from the position of victim to creator.

Inevitably, the years impose themselves, as I note in my little book, *I Grow Old Therefore I Am,* and my carcass is weighed down despite my best efforts and care. But my rage to live is unchanged...

28
Sin

Without having The Answer to my spiritual question, I've nevertheless received a few clues that temper my obsession, the origins of which go back to my grandfather André's anxieties.

The first was given to me in the 1980s at the Saint Maire parish in Lausanne by Father Jacques Goettmann, then an Orthodox priest in Buenos Aires. He was giving a lecture there. After listening to my question, he abruptly turned around.

Not a word.

This puny man remained in this posture for a long time:

His back turned...

This symbolic gesture will forever mark my vision of sin. The spiritual, the psychological, the social, even the political.

The second will always be that of Metropolitan Hierotheos with his image of the heart buried beneath ashes. Of the relationship between our battles against our inner thoughts, whatever they may be, and our supplication to the Holy Spirit.

The third was during my confessions at the Saint Joseph parish in Bordeaux, with Father Marc, now Monsignor Marc. Because he knew how to place my delusions not before a man, but before the God who experienced the source of our temptations of the flesh.

Finally, the fourth, from a brother monk's persistent challenge, each time I return to the heart of the Troodos:

"Are you suffocating, Maria? Are you no longer breathing?"

For him and all the monks, breathing means hammering out the prayer of the heart:

"Lord Jesus Christ, Son of God, have mercy on me!"

The vacuum cleaner of the heart's filth so that Mercy can slip in.

But... but also, once again, it's not a magic formula or a miraculous click! Every time I force myself to repeat it, the lid of the boiling pot explodes. And piles of suggestions, not necessarily bad, parade through my soul. Assail me. Sometimes exhaust me. To get rid of them, there is only dialogue with others. The friend, or my superior, the therapist, who pins multitudes of butterflies to the walls, inviting me to observe them with detachment. Or even the confessor. As long as confession doesn't adhere to a moralising script but tries hard to free the soul of its parasites. The difference? For me, an Orthodox Christian, the priest who stands before the icon of the greatest therapist and exorcist, Christ, is a "consecrated channel" for the flow of divine energy. Energy which – and this is where it differs from psychotherapy – confers the sacrament of forgiveness. Embedding the awareness that there is a mafia of "demons" who oppose it. Beginning with my own foolishness, as imperious as it is talkative. And then those ancestral knots lodged in my unconscious that I have tried to untie.

Finally...

One only has to look at history, including the contemporary, so-called modern era, to be convinced:

The Empire of Darkness. That wants to impose its reign of division. Of turning our backs on others. Of hatred and chaos. This empire with which churches have often joined forces, to enslave and terrorise souls. When they weren't also destroying bodies. Which was, and is, undoubtedly the greatest of victories for the one who was the first to turn his back on the Other.

I remember, during an ECOF (Orthodox Catholic Church of France) general meeting, a personal question from a soul-searching friend, to which Monsignor Germain replied:

"Sometimes in life, an angel pushes you to do something. And you don't always know if it's an angel of God or an angel of Satan..."

It's why the correct original Greek translation of the Lord's Prayer is not "Deliver us from evil." From a vague and abstract evil, but:

"Deliver us from the Evil One!"

I dare add, since I've experienced it, that this same Evil One is clever enough to draw me into reciting a mantra to dry out my heart. I pray, therefore I love! Not at all! I pray and I am dry...

A dry heart, that feels justified in its arrogant dearth of humility!

Monsignor Germain liked to repeat to us:

"Do everything not to damage your heart!"

So many traps... so much tenderness too...

Last, I want to add to the list another form of subtle deviation:

Self-destruction:

While passing through tunnels so gloomy that we turn our backs on our own bodies. The most dreadful for me was when Laurent was hospitalised with leukaemia, just after going through my parents' last breaths. I was getting bogged down, literally and figuratively, on the verge of giving up. One day, I was having tea in the station buffet of the watchmaking diocese. The one that had seen me parade as the beauty queen on a flower-covered float. I no longer had the ability to dress decently or wash my hair. Then a man in rags with a greasy ponytail entered. He was leaning on a walking stick as he went to the bar. Then he saw me and limped over to me:

"Madam, is it okay if I keep you company?"

My market value of car and luxury villa had just

suffered the biggest crash. It couldn't have fallen any lower! It was an electric shock that left me in pieces, if I hadn't been shattered already. What have you become, my hobo angel? Do you wash your clothes and hair with those budget products that cost the same as that drink you wanted to offer me? To bring under your wing a capsized accomplice? In any case, I thank you for shaking me up without you knowing it, reminding me that nothing justifies wasting energy...

29

My Protector Myth

Sometimes I think about the *chance* happenings that allowed me to write these lines. What part does *providence* play in these sparks of *good fortune?* Everyone will have their own answers, based on their own lives. Their own truths. Unique. I searched for mine, and they were often very different. Finally, I settled on a personal choice, my "protector myth," so to speak:

My guardian angel is wonderful!

He has the added advantage of not being an idea, a concept. I consider him a character. Better still, a person I can address. A person I can love...

In my monastery in Cyprus, at the entrance to the courtyard, there is a moving depiction of death. Death, my long-time enemy:

Death arrives with his scythe to tear a woman

from her bed. The demons at the foot of the bed stir, but her guardian angel comes to retrieve the woman's soul, represented by the woman in miniature. She joins a long procession where other deceased people are walking. Everywhere there are barriers. The demons who, while we are alive, push us, through distractions, away from a divine life, are now gathering together those same distractions to form a roadblock. The guardian angel encourages, argues, and helps the little soul to move forward. Until the moment when she arrives before Christ's throne. It is there that the guardian angel releases the woman. She must advance alone. Both hands joined, she approaches, then kneels before the King of Forgiveness and Love. And it is before this King that my heart has finally chosen to bow. Right now, on this earth. Abandoning all that spiritual Don Juanism to kneel in turn before this God-Made-Man and this Man-Made-God. A choice made freely. Not from any fanaticism and self-reliance. Just a free choice of love before the Fiancé of my wounded soul...

Every time I enter my monastery, I stand frozen before this painting. I never tire of it. It inspires me. It becomes engraved in me...

So, the crazy person that I still am, asks her guardian angel every morning not only to continue protecting her, but also to accompany her at the hour of her death...

If possible, not right away:

Every time I emerge from the ocean, hands in their swim paddles, I lift my head – a little more screwed on – high towards the sky:

"Lord, I still have such a desire to live! To pray. To commune. To write.

To love..."

Epilogue

This tangle of words that Mireille had hoped to start writing a few years ago has become an inner journey. Therapy even. Temporarily at least, nothing is ever definitively acquired. It has allowed me to clear out the weeds. To dig. To meditate. A story that has become mine, and from which I have retained a part of a secret garden that will remain so, even for curious friends! On the other hand, if one of my readers feels the urge to tackle their own story, I can only encourage them to do so. I have not invented any episode. No encounter. I have consciously veiled the darker sides of the characters I've included. So as not to reveal what chance or my intuition had exposed. Especially since the majority of those shadows are lurking within me. I hold fast to this saint's recommendation, that Monsignor Germain shared with us:

"When you are shocked by the fault in your

neighbour, immediately ask God for forgiveness, for it means that the fault lies dormant deep within you!"

However, I sincerely ask forgiveness from those to whom my words or omissions could have caused hurt. This was never my intention!

I have tried to recount things faithfully. Including, as I recently said to a stunned Parisian writer, that:

"In the end, we are all puppets!"

More or less falling apart. I'm also sure that I need the perspective of others to rebuild myself. But accepting this loss of face gives me a precious autonomy. Tightrope walking requires carefully measured steps. I am convinced that nothing is ever done entirely freely. Neither for the devoted priest, humbly pinned to his cassock, nor even for the saint working primarily for the salvation of his soul. For me, a Christian, or someone who thinks I am, there is only the Master who, despite his most human inherent fear, took a beating for free. Who, amidst the spitting and whipping, freely climbed onto the wood of the cross. Forgiving "those who know not what they do". This forgiveness so divinely His...

So I have eliminated accusation, revenge, and judgment. So that my story may be transfigured into "reconciliation", to borrow Boris Cyrulnik's words. This is what sometimes happened when I abandoned my illusions about myself. Some rekindled wounds are not healed. But I feel there is a boundary beyond which, as my friend Dr. François Marie Tanazacq, who encouraged me to keep on with this book, says: "We must stop picking at the scabs!" Even those that, underneath, are still festering. There's no sticking plaster for everything! I want to avoid, if possible, getting bogged down in the obsession with Cartesian or not-so-Cartesian elucidations, delving into the consequences of every wound on the body or soul. I believe that sometimes chance, bad luck, genetics, about which we know so much, also have their place. I prefer to move forward. Move forward with this shield that can be summed up in three words:

Sincerity, sincerity, sincerity.

The same goes for the unconscious traumas that I, like everyone else, have carried around for generations. Family memory mired in that unclear zone that often only asks to remain so. Here too, I have drawn a line at archaeological excavations of the past. The simple past and the anterior past. Accepting the need to open myself up to my destiny, because not all mysteries can be solved. This book is also a tribute to my ancestors, my dear parents, and my Laurent, whom I miss. But also to all those I have encountered. They all have a place in my prayers. Those who are still alive, as well as those who have gone, many of them in atheism. Not so that Christ will greet them as beaten down slaves. He, better than anyone, honours our freedom. Even the freedom to turn our backs on Him. But so that they, in turn, might have the desire to kneel before the King of Reconciliation…

This book is also the culmination of rigorous work to manage the time and energy without which nothing is possible. It has brought its share of insomnia, painful bouts of gastritis, restlessness, and sometimes tears. But the more the words escape, reveal themselves, or correct themselves, the more I become a spectator. The spectator of a path both "imposed" and chosen. Built through encounters. One determination after another to rise again by accepting the hand being extended to me. And this gives my weakened frame a kind of liberation. I can feel even more how much certain knots had just needed to be untied. Without any pretension, with my white head neither too high nor too low and my legs wrapped in support stockings, I feel that these knots are not limited to me. Nor only to this world to which, thanks to the intercessions of my wonderful guardian angel, I still belong. But they have even managed to be untied in the other world. The invisible one just as full and just as present. It's called the onset of madness. Or faith. Or exaltation. Or simply another expression of communion. It's up to each of us to sort that for ourselves!

In all sincerity...

This reconciliation has led to a literary epilogue. Marking the end of a collection of writings centred essentially on my intimate experiences. Opening the next door, into my first "freely-inspired" novel. Even if inspiration is always intertwined with what has imbued our souls. This time, I'm planning for my protagonist to be a man...

I've also been led through greater lucidity to reconcile myself with my limits. Although I pray for those who have hurt me or hurt those I love, which, first and foremost, sends its positive energies to my soul, from now on I won't be associating with them. Preserving my vitality and my health for less energy-consuming and toxic encounters.

I do what I can. Everyone does what they can. With their bruises.

The other goes his or her way. With the others...

For me, feeling grateful for *destiny* or the *destined* means recognising its mystery. Confining myself to honing my own inner deliverance by augmenting life's freedoms.

"To go deeper into ourselves so that we can accommodate the other." With a benevolent reverence for the uniqueness of the Person.

I am a million miles away from holding a permanent subscription to serenity:

Anger and resentment are catching up with me. Envy. The desire to be able to open my purse and treat myself to one of those luxury spas people go to when they're bored to death. But where my arthritic frame would be well cared for. Still, neither the car nor the luxury villa seems that appealing if you've already died of boredom...

Often anxieties, old ones or new just-as-insidious ones, make themselves known. Sadness at the thought of that family that is no longer there, or the one I don't have ahead of me...

So, I follow the advice of my lovely editor, translator, and English friend, Jacqueline:

"Take a deep breath and have a cup of tea!"

And when I drink my tea, I remember the herbal teas at the monastery with our Geronda Athanasios. Because in the very heart of our conversations, and especially in his sacred silences, those enriched by eight decades of asceticism, I managed to capture serenity. The serenity of his breath:

"Lord Jesus Christ, Son of God, have mercy on me!"

Biel, December 4, 2024, feast of Saint Barbara and the 30th anniversary of the death of Dr. Dietmar Pfister.

English translation completed on Easter Monday, 2025.

www.ingramcontent.com/pod-product-compliance
Lightning Source LLC
Chambersburg PA
CBHW020407080526
44584CB00014B/1213